Endorsements

"Beautifully vulnerable."

Mary E. DeMuth
Author of *The Wall Around Your Heart,*
Not Marked, and *Thin Places*

"This is an excellent read that will touch your heart and enlighten your mind."

Regina Stone Matthews
Speaker and Award-Winning Children's Book Author
of the *When I Dream* series and *Words and Actions*

"This story, in all its detail, is a picture of the challenges, heartaches, and blessings of pursuing a dream, guided by the hand of God."

Nancy Johnson
Member of the Davis Life Group at
Lake Pointe Church Firewheel, Garland, Texas

"Rachelle's story shows a woman who loves our Savior, her husband, her children and three children in a faraway country who had no family. The journey was tedious and heart-breaking, but her tenacity was based on the truths God gave her through each step. Truth, faith, and love equal 'family.'"

Martha Gallion
Member of the Davis Life Group at Lake Pointe Church Firewheel,
Garland, Texas, Fellow Adoptive mother

Painful Waiting

Leaning On God Through
Yet Another Adoption Process

Rachelle D. Alspaugh

AUTHENTICITY
BOOK HOUSE

Painful Waiting:Leaning on God through yet Another Adoption Process
From the Surviving the Valley series

Copyright © 2016 by Rachelle D. Alspaugh
ISBN: 978-1-943004-07-2 (Paperback)

Cover designed by Joanna Martin

Published by Authenticity Book House

Printed in the United States of America

10 9 8 7 6 5 4 3 2 1

AUTHENTICITY
BOOK HOUSE

Authenticity Book House
c/o Proven Way Ministries
The Hope Center
2001 W. Plano Parkway, Suite 3422
Plano, TX 75075 USA

Dedication

For my husband, Mike, and his courage to climb the mountain again for the sake of our boys.

For our three boys, the treasures of my heart. I love all of you and am grateful for you.

For Scott and Oscar, only God could orchestrate the connections with both of you.

For Mercedes, it was an absolute Diosidencia to find you. I am so eternally grateful God crossed our paths.

For Zayde, you are an amazing gift of friendship.

For Martha, your encouragement and your constant support held me together.

For the Davis Life Group, thank you for five long years of support, always believing in us and God's purposes for our family.

For my late Grandfather, Jack Greener, thank you for your faithfulness to pray for me every single day for many years. Not a day goes by that I am not grateful for those prayers.

For my Grandmother, Alice Greener, thank you for modeling a real-life love relationship with Jesus.

For my parents, Karl and Priscilla Kloppmann, thank you for cheering me on as a writer.

Table of Contents

Introduction

A closed door. One earlier slammed in our face. Did we dare turn the knob? Did we actually consider trying to walk through it again?

Our family attempted to adopt two siblings from Colombia in 2008, a seven-year-old girl, Viviana, and her eleven-year-old brother, Juan David. We blindly walked through the entire adoption process for them, as long and tedious as it was (not to mention costly), only to run straight into a wall, a dead end. Shock, bewilderment, humiliation, and guilt followed us for nearly a year afterward.

We made all preparations for the arrival of those two precious Colombian siblings in our home, yet only empty rooms and beds remained. Closets full of clothing selected specifically for each child silently screamed in our faces every time we walked by them. Their absence left an awkward hollowness in our lives, one that no one understood, considering they were never our children in the first place. We still grieved as if we'd experienced a death in the family, even though they never even lived in our home.

Our seven-year-old biological son, David, responded with incredible anger—toward Colombia for allowing its professionals to so misjudge his parents and toward God for not letting his siblings come home. Only three years had passed since God took his only biological sibling home to heaven via a miscarried pregnancy.

In the midst of our grieving, we found grace in the most unexpected way. We found the son God meant us to find: Julian, the older sibling of the two children we lost. He found his way into our lives at the age of sixteen, and we finally met him face to face in Colombia soon after his eighteenth birthday.

As much as we loved his siblings, we knew they still had a chance to join a family. He didn't. His age prevented him from finding a family of his own. He saw nothing but a bleak, lonely future—without his siblings, without his mother, without a soul to claim him. I say we found *him*, but he actually found *us*. We both experienced a miracle when God divinely crossed our paths.

We accepted it as our story. Embraced it. I recounted the entire experience of grief, loss, grace, and healing in my first book, *Unexpected Tears*. God prepared to write more in our story, though, showing us that closed doors mean nothing to him. We never dreamed how he would use that divine connection he'd given us to Julian.

Only by turning the knob and walking through the door *again* could our family finally find closure to that painful, bewildering chapter of our lives. After we obediently took that first step, we let God take us by the hand for the remainder of the journey where he led us from the mountaintop to the valley and back to the mountaintop *again*.

What we let go, he gave back. And more.
He indeed restored the years the locusts had eaten
(Joel 2:25).

Part One

FROM THE MOUNTAINTOP . . .

1

A NEW PURPOSE, A NEW SONG

"He put a new song in my mouth, a hymn of
praise to our God."
Psalm 40:3a

The Magic in Your Eyes

So many priceless memories made
Such miraculous moments in time
Each step worth it all,
Every bit of our climb.

Gazing now upon each picture
I'm greeted by surprise
The biggest miracle I see is
The transformation in your eyes.

The very first moment we captured
Your eyes show me a bit of fear
They tell me you are nervous
Yet relieved we're finally near.

After a few days together
Your eyes tell me you feel right at home
You look so happy to be with us
Rather than talking over a phone.

Soon I see your eyes begin dancing
I see a sparkle not evident before.
Every expression of love for you
Makes them shine even more.

We witnessed many miracles
So many dreams come true
But the change in your eyes was like magic
Over those fourteen days with you.

Wow! Fourteen days. Fourteen life-changing days in a country I'd once given up on seeing, spent with people I thought we never stood a chance to meet. Now more than a thousand pictures sat on my laptop, waiting for me to sift through each one, to relive each moment. Constant tears streamed down my cheeks for days on end. Tears of joy and gratitude mixed with tears of sadness. I missed him.

Life suddenly held new meaning and hope as we finally experienced that tender closure to such a heart-breaking experience. We found our son, he found his family. Julian. We could've wallowed in bitterness for years and chosen to turn our backs on Colombia like the Adoption Committee turned their back on us. Instead we chose to believe there remained a story yet to be revealed. I'm so thankful we didn't give up believing Colombia still held treasures for us to find.

Isn't it like God to prescribe exactly what we need to fill the empty holes in our lives? Who better could understand what we lost than the brother who lost them, too? Who better to embrace Julian as a son than someone who knew and loved his siblings, someone who wanted to keep his memories of them alive, cherishing each one?

We'd barely been home a day or two, yet I couldn't waste a single moment without immediately sifting through the thousand plus pictures we caught on camera. For as long as we waited to finally experience Colombia's beauty, we tried to capture each and every moment. We didn't want to miss a thing or take the chance of forgetting even a minute of our adventure or our time with Julian.

This proved to be no simple task. Our pictures represented more than simple snapshots of the places we visited and people we spent time with. They were more than candid moments showing off each adventure we experienced as a family. I knew they told a story, so I tediously organized and sequenced them in a way to give the story justice. Our story, one of loss and failure later claimed as victory—Julian's story, one of abandonment and fear turned to hope and belonging.

As I sat there with my computer open, I cropped each picture carefully to express the right mood and personality of the scene. I didn't expect to see what God revealed to me in those pictures. When I cropped them and put them in proper sequence, I soon saw magic dance before me. Those eyes, those beautiful eyes. Julian's eyes magically transformed during our time spent together, growing in warmth and intensity with each day that passed.

I will always remember the first moment we met Julian, a joyous yet awkward moment. We got to know each other quite well during the previous year via telephone and online conversation, but we'd never once seen each other face to face. A handful of pictures posted online gave us a chance to see what the other one looked like.

I learned to read his mood and emotion in each picture by the expression in his eyes. It always surprised him when he sent me a random picture via the computer, and I immediately sensed his mood. He'd ask how I saw sadness if his mouth held a smile or how I detected joy if a smile could not be found. Easily. I read it in his eyes. They spoke a language of their own.

For months before we headed to Colombia, I could hardly wait until our eyes finally met. Yet when the day actually arrived, we felt a mutual anxiety to meet each other. Now, as I relived those first moments and hours by studying the pictures in front of me, that nervousness really stood out. His eyes seemed glazed over, showing him question if this scenario was too good to be true.

Had *his* family finally come for him? Did he really get onto a bus with us, not to return to his home in the orphanage for two whole weeks? Nearly an adult already, he knew he trusted too many people in his lifetime, people who later turned around and let him down. Would this time be the same? It was all there, written in his eyes, so incredibly apparent in each picture we continuously snapped over those first few days.

I continued to sort through all the pictures, putting them in chronological order, while I watched those eyes soften within the first few days. They grew warmer, showing his growing level of comfort. He enjoyed his time with us and trusted us. He felt at home, and he knew we were for real. We weren't going to turn around and abandon him. Though still hesitant to really shine, Julian trusted he was in a good, safe place with people who truly cared about him. His smile held a gentle warmth, matching the expression in his eyes.

Over the days that followed in the photographs, those eyes showed me a new and growing confidence. We earned more of his trust each day, and he gradually let down his guard. In the pictures taken toward the middle of our trip, I saw more than warmth, comfort, and confidence in his eyes. I saw a sparkle in them, one that seemed to dance with a new light in his eyes.

I'll never forget those beautiful moments when he looked me in the eye and gave me one of the most gorgeous smiles I'd ever seen.

"I am having a wonderful time with you!" He enjoyed each and every moment with us. His eyes twinkled with delight. I didn't realize the pictures captured it too. Even if he wanted to hide his true feelings, his eyes couldn't lie.

A teardrop now escaped the corner of my own eye as I recalled one of those painfully rewarding moments between me and God shortly before we embarked on our journey to Colombia. Pictures of Juan David and Viviana, Julian's younger siblings, still covered the walls in our home. Even after the adoption pursuit failed, I couldn't bear to take the pictures down because I promised Juan David I never would. Those two children meant so much to me, to us, and I knew there had to be a purpose not yet revealed, a story not yet told. Taking them down meant accepting the end to our story, admitting it was all a mistake.

"Viviana is now home with her new Mommy in Europe. Juan David is not, nor will he ever be my son. They are forever Julian's siblings. Those pictures belong with him." They didn't belong to me. I reluctantly rehearsed the truth aloud while I rode my bike one evening late in May.

I bravely and tearfully took each picture down from the wall and placed them all in a folder for Julian. I knew those pictures would mean so much to him. I had yet to learn he didn't even own a single printed picture of his siblings. Taking them down was more painful than I wanted to admit, but it also felt good to know even those pictures held a purpose. Now a gift for Julian, one he would treasure even more than I did while I owned them.

I thought it would be harder than ever to come home to those empty picture frames, accepting the closure I wasn't sure I wanted. Yet now I saw it so clearly. Our new pictures of Julian, our family of four, now replaced the pictures of his siblings. I needed a place to display those beautiful, magical eyes.

Julian's pictures soon covered the walls of our home, reminding us daily of the new song God put in our heart, the beauty he created out of our broken pieces.

2

SPREADING THEIR VOICE

"Truly I tell you, whatever you did for one of the least of these
brothers and sisters of mine, you did for me."
Matthew 25:40

Love Me as I Am

An orphan is what they call me
An unlucky child, some may say.
I grew up without a family,
Now I'm just trying to find my way.

You may be tempted to judge me,
You may think I'm immature for my age,
I think I've done pretty well
For being raised in an orphanage.

Of course you'll find gaps in my life.
There's so much I never learned,
Things I never had a chance to practice,
Or times I never got my turn.

Still I am who I am today
Because of my unique experiences in life,
I faced more loss than most ever do,
I conquered incredible internal strife.

Please don't try to change me.
I'm not a project for you to fix.
Please love me as I am
Without trying to alter the mix.

I can add so much to the world,
And love to the moon and beyond,
But 'til I know you truly love me,
My heart won't ever respond.

So, our adoption story took a different turn than expected. We became Julian's "unofficial" family, giving our lives a whole new purpose. I felt joy in my heart again. Sadly, we could never make the arrangement legal. Julian already passed the allowable age for an international adoption into the United States. Colombia's Adoption Committee officially closed its doors to us, anyway. Once they reject you, they don't allow you to try again. God strategically used Julian to keep us tied to such a beautiful country rather than running as far away as possible. Colombia offered even more than we witnessed over those first fourteen days.

By accepting this new story that somehow embraced three orphan's lives but did not include an adoption, we realized God looked at a different agenda. A new passion stirred within our hearts.

We knew too much. We saw too much. We heard too much. We'd been too involved in their lives to stay silent.

Julian's siblings' voices replayed constantly in my head. I still heard the longing and the heartache every time I tried to say good-bye over the phone, the hurt I sensed whenever they asked why I didn't call. They loved and cherished us as dearly as we loved and cherished them. I couldn't erase the images of all we saw within that orphanage, the looks in the children's eyes. I couldn't ignore their stories.

"Write it down, dear child. Write it down." I heard the tender whisper as clearly as if he'd shouted in my ear.

I knew what I needed to do. I'd never make sense of our entire experience over the last three years if I didn't try to write it out. Yet I also knew the price attached to doing so. In my grief, I placed that whole box up on the shelf, hoping to never bring it back down until I could emotionally handle it. I buried so many emotions over those three years, along with all of the poetry I wrote throughout the entire adoption process. Fear gripped my heart at the thought of bringing the box down to face the heart-wrenching contents.

I finally understood how people can suppress memories because I suppressed so many of my own. Taking the time and energy to write it all down meant facing it all again. I had to feel it. I needed to grieve. Yet somehow God filled me with the strength to bring that box down and pull the contents out.

Once I started to write, I couldn't stop. It poured out of me. I held nothing back. Poetry I wrote to and about those sweet children now found its place on my page. Oh, how I wished they knew what tender words I penned for them throughout our unsuccessful pursuit to bring them home.

God taught me so much about their desires and their longings. He never meant for me to bury it all deep inside me or stuff it into a box to sit on a shelf. He gave me intimate insight into three orphan's lives, representing millions of others like them all over the globe. I couldn't get their voices out of my head because God wanted me to let others hear them, too.

Viviana taught me how much an orphan wants to be important to someone. I'll never forget the way she squealed with delight every time she heard my voice. My phone calls to her let her know someone thought she was special. While we talked for fifteen to thirty minutes each week, she held all of my attention. She didn't need to blend in with a crowd, and she loved every second of it.

She often begged her house parent to let her stay up later than the other girls so she didn't miss hearing my voice over the phone. On the occasions when I called too late in the evening, someone would wake her from her sleep so she could talk to me. When you live in a house with twenty-seven little girls, most of whom do not receive phone calls, your weekly phone call is like your twenty minutes of fame. She found every excuse in the book to not let me say good-bye. I showered her with precious words of love through every single call.

Personal wants and desires filled that little girl's heart, and she knew I wanted to know everything about her. When we think of meeting an orphan's needs, we tend to think of how we might meet their physical and even emotional needs. Yet these kids possess individual desires that fit their personalities, like any other child, hoping for a specific color, toy, or animal.

It speaks volumes when you'll go out of your way to get exactly what they want. She wanted an orange blanket, a puppy, and purple sunglasses. (She never came home to the orange blanket we bought for her, but we did send her the stuffed white puppy and purple sunglasses at Christmastime.) More than knowing we loved her, she knew we saw her and heard her.

Juan David taught me how much an orphan wants to be loved and cherished, how much he longs to be part of a family. It took time to earn his trust, but once earned, I needn't fear losing it. It took him a while to believe me when I said I loved him, to believe I didn't speak empty words. Yet the consistency of my phone calls to both him and his sister proved my commitment to them, and I soon won his heart.

He looked forward to all of my phone calls, and he, too, waited up for them. He let me know how much he missed talking to me whenever something prevented me from calling him.

"I was sad on Friday when you didn't call me. You know how much your calls mean to me and how much I enjoy talking to you." I'll never forget the longing I heard in those words after I didn't call one particular evening. Those twenty minutes on the phone, in the midst of twenty-seven other boys, spoke one thing. Somebody cared about *him*. Somebody loved *him*.

Julian unexpectedly opened my eyes to the orphan crisis even more than the other two. You hear stories about the kids all the time, the ones growing up without families. An orphanage is no place to call home, and it deprives them of so many social and emotional needs. But time still remains to make a difference in their lives. Many still have a chance at adoption. So many programs exist to raise money and awareness for their needs. They may be considered the "forgotten" children, but at least someone meets their immediate needs for food and shelter.

Yet how often do you hear the voices of the ones that ran out of time? How often do you hear the voices of the orphans who aged out of the system and stepped into life alone? It happens every day. I know the heartache involved because we walked Julian through the terrifying process of walking away from the one place he called home for so many years. Even if it never felt like home to him, his needs were always met. Then he suddenly found himself completely lost and alone. Sadly, we lived 2,500 miles away on another continent and couldn't get back for another four months.

"I need to buy a mattress. Where do I go? How much does it cost?" I heard the anguish in his voice as he typed those words to me.

We found someone to help with the mattress and delivery, but the panicked conversations continued.

"I need to go to the store to buy food. I don't know where to go. What should I buy? What can I make? How do I make it? Please help me! Tell me what to do." Anxiety gripped him over basic living skills.

The gaps I saw in this precious young man's life were far wider than I ever presumed. The government met his physical needs over all these years. He completed his education plus a year of technical school. Great psychologists, social workers, and even a nutritionist worked with him. Yet he didn't have a clue how to cook, how to shop, how to budget, or even how to eat properly. He didn't know how to ration his food or eat nutritionally. He didn't know how to save or manage money, compare prices, or plan ahead.

He didn't get to make a lot of choices in the orphanage, so he developed this "learned helplessness" because of his circumstances. No one ever gave him much of a chance to step up and take charge of himself. There are life skills you learn and practice in a home with a family that you don't learn when you're in a house with twenty-seven other youth.

My heart broke when I realized that once Julian stepped out of that orphanage, he had no home to ever go back to. He didn't have a chance to feel the waters, to gradually taste independence before fully embracing it. He went from having all of his needs met and choices made for him to having to meet every one of his needs and make every choice for himself completely on his own.

In our own culture, most eighteen-year-old children first test the waters of independence. Yet they know they can always go back home on the weekend to ask for guidance. They can still lean on Mom and Dad for financial advice and support. They can usually find a place at home to crash for a while in order to get back on their feet.

Julian didn't have that option. Gaps or not, he couldn't go back home because no home, or family, existed to go back to.

Eighteen Years

Eighteen years old,
Ready to spread their wings,
Ready to face the world
While in pursuit of their dreams.

"I'm ready for this challenge,
I'm prepared for the task ahead.
I'm ready to face the obstacles.
Free at last!" they said.

Yet eighteen years didn't quite prepare them,
Eighteen years of training weren't enough.
The world held more than they bargained for.
Life on their own was rough.

Grateful for parents who loved them,
Grateful for a place to call home,
They returned to a place of security,
Finding the street no place to roam.

Yet what if it wasn't that easy,
And eighteen years were all you got?
Once you reach that magic age,
You survive alone on what you were taught.

No material possessions to take with you,
No family to call on for support,
No home to ever go back to,
No place to find security or resort.

What if you were the orphan
Left to figure out life on your own?
Please listen to their voices
So one less faces this picture alone.

We heard the terror and anxiety in his voice. We felt the hopelessness he carried as he stepped into the future alone. Yet none of that compared to the ache in his heart from losing his siblings. No one ever gave him a chance to grieve for them.

The heartbreaking truth is that siblings are split all the time. Sometimes it's the only way. Better to find a separate family for each one, or even just for one, than to let them all grow up without families. Sometimes, they never even get to say good-bye.

Rather than cherishing his final night with his sister, Julian did not even have permission to see her the day before she left with her new adoptive mother. Actually, they spent very little time together while the Adoption Committee searched for a family for her.

"It's better not to get too attached. The separation will be too hard later." That's what his psychologist told him, but I'm not sure I agree with her reasoning.

He didn't need to say anything at all. We heard the anguish in his heart loud and clear. Eighteen years old, raised in an institution. He stayed close to his siblings for many years, yet now he lived completely estranged from both of them as he faced the world alone. His time came, yet he lost all contact with his sister and had no authorization to communicate with his brother. Viviana lived somewhere in Europe with a teacher who adopted her, and Juan David lived with a local family whom he assumed would adopt him soon.

Julian didn't even own a single picture of the three of them together. In fact, the only pictures he even owns of them now are the ones God burdened my heart to give him. The only tangible memories he holds of his little sister are a tiny stuffed bear she gave him and a stuffed duck she had owned. My heart hurts for him when I see him hold that little bear close to his heart, knowing the gaping hole her absence left there.

I finally got it. I heard the Author of this story whisper again into my ear.

"My child, I know this hurts. I didn't burden your heart for them or give you the chance to love and be loved by them only for you to bury it all inside. Write it down. Give them a voice. Speak for these children and the millions they represent. What you learned from them is not common knowledge. It is a gift I entrusted to you, a gift I chose to give others *through you*."

Have You Heard?

Have you heard the voice of the orphan?
Do you know the sound of his cries?
Do you know what life has done to him
As he wonders where his future lies?

Have you felt his broken heart
When his mother never came back around?
Have you wiped away his tears
When his dreams crashed to the ground?

Were you there when they told him
the days would only be few
Before they took away his flesh and blood,
Taking his sister out of view?

Do you see his empty eyes
As he longs to hear her voice again?
Can you fill the gaping hole
where her presence had always been?

Do you wonder how he does it,
Waiting to see what each day will bring?
Sometimes an opportunity to grasp,
Sometimes another painful sting.

Do you imagine what he goes through,
As he steps into life alone?
Can you suppress his fears
As he faces each unknown?

Have you held him in your arms,
As the tears stream down his cheek,
Knowing you are leaving him
With a future that still looks bleak?

Have you watched him pray at night,
As he lets the tears just flow,
Begging God to bring his mama back,
Yet knowing it would never be so?

Have you heard her stall your conversation,
Cherishing every word you said,
Not wanting you to say good-bye,
Before her time to go to bed?

Have you heard the cry of the orphan
And wonder what you can do?
Have you ever wondered if
That orphan had been you?

Christmas as an Orphan

Now that Christmas has arrived again,
The gifts have all been given,
We enjoy a quiet peace,
Reflecting on our Gift from heaven.

I enjoy a morning cup of coffee,
My husband reads beside the fire,
My son still slumbers in his bed,
The dogs have once again retired.

There is a warm and cozy feeling,
The kind only a family can bring.
Makes me wonder what it's like for you
Spending Christmas in an orphanage.

Is there a warm and cozy feeling,
In your home of twenty-seven boys?
Do you feel loved and cherished,
Is your home filled with all new toys?

I can only imagine the longing
Tucked deep inside your heart,
Wishing you'd spent Christmas with our family
Rather than over a thousand miles apart.

I wonder if once again you fought the feeling
That God forgot all about you
As you spent this first Christmas apart
From the only family you ever knew.

Christmas Without Her

I thought I was the one grieving,
But my loss truly can't compare
To how your heart aches now,
This first Christmas without her there.

Despite knowing she's happy with a family,
To you, it's like she disappeared.
They took her from your life,
And broke all communication, as you feared.

How you long to hear her voice,
To look again into her eyes.
How you miss her tender hugs,
And wish you could have said good-bye.

What can I do to ease your hurting?
What can I do to dull your pain?
I'm so sorry for all you've suffered
For her brighter future to be gained.

Know that God is with her,
Wherever she may be today,
And know his arms are holding you,
Throughout this painful holiday.

Know that you are cherished,
You are loved beyond compare,
Know my heart is with you,
Wishing we were there.

3

THE DESIRE OF MY HEART

"Delight yourself in the Lord, and He will give you
the desires of your heart."
Psalm 37:4

Consumed

Satisfied . . .
That's what I prayed to be,
Satisfied with his love
And the daily mercies given to me.

I wanted nothing else to matter,
No desire to even come close
To the satisfaction I so often find
When his Presence in me shows.

Yet when I'm merely satisfied,
My heart can grow content.
I expect the same each day
And miss out on his greater intent.

I remain where I am, stuck in a rut,
Seeing only as much as I've seen before.
Yet he desires every last part of me
So he can give me even more.

So satisfied I no longer am
Until I'm filled to the brim.
I want my life to clearly show
I'm completely consumed by him.

Life handed us many opportunities the last few years to fret and worry about things we could not control. We spent more than a year of our lives pouring our every ounce of energy into a pursuit that would later crumble before our eyes. All the time, energy, money, and emotion wasted, or so it seemed.

Then came the bewildering moments, hours and days where we did nothing but stare off into space, wondering how we could have been so convinced, so misled. Countless questions without answers. How did we move on?

We wanted to seek direction, but we didn't know how. Utterly convinced God directed us to pursue the adoption, we didn't quite understand this dead end. After the fact, we desperately wanted to know where to turn, what direction to go, who to talk to, how to cope, and how to move on.

No more checklists guided our every step or drove our daily actions. Those lists gave us a sense of security, leading us somewhere. What now? What next? What an incredibly empty, bewildering feeling.

I relived it all. Writing it down hurt. I didn't even know if I could finish. I felt the tension rise within me the closer I got to the part in the story where everything fell apart. Would I fall apart with it?

Then I heard that tender whisper again.

"Stop searching, child. Stop looking for answers and for direction. Stop trying to figure out which way to turn, which path to take, or which way to go. Seek *me*, my child. Seek *me*. I am all you need. I am the answer you seek. I am the way. I am the direction you need to go. I am the path you are to take. When you seek *me*, I will be the answer you need."

By seeking *him* instead of an answer to all my questions, I gained a whole new outlook and perspective on our circumstance. Instead of asking which way to turn next, I gained a new way of living, one consumed with knowing him over everything else. Knowing him more intimately gave me incredible peace and contentment while everyone around me pushed us to keep fighting back.

"Isn't there a part of you that still wants to go straight to the people who denied you and ask why?" We'd made it all the way to Colombia, and now my newest friend, Clarita, asked me the same question that haunted me for so long.

"No. There's not." I remember the conversation as clearly as I remember my response.

Honestly, when God asks you to let something go, he gives you the strength to do it. I no longer desired to know. The question didn't consume me anymore. I didn't need answers. God gave me closure to our story when he gave us Julian. That was enough for me.

"Father, satisfy me with your presence." I prayed every morning to find myself completely satisfied with Christ so nothing else could scream for my attention. By letting go of the constant questions and need to know why, I found freedom. But God wanted to take me further. He took me higher yet, teaching me that satisfaction is not enough. I needed to be more than satisfied with his love. He wanted to consume me.

Everything would change from that point on. Everything. My plans. My schedule. My finances. My prayer life. Even my hopes and dreams. Letting God consume me meant letting go of myself and my pride.

I'm a private person. I'm the quiet one in a crowd. I don't share much when I'm in a group. I'm the listener, not the talker. Very few people ever really get to know me. Yet as I wrote down our story, I laid my heart bare on every page. I stopped hiding.

With each suppressed memory and emotion I wrote came an overwhelming sense of peace, healing, and closure to such a painful chapter in my life. I stuffed the whole experience so deeply inside me, hoping to never face it again. I didn't talk about it to anyone, meaning I never processed any of those emotions. Facing it now, after all this time, surprisingly brought healing, meaning, and purpose.

"If I ever write a book someday, I want to fill it with my poetry. A book of poems with a story behind each poem." I smiled as I remembered sharing those thoughts with a group of fourth-grade students many years ago. Without even planning it, that's exactly how our story looked when I finally put the period on the last page.

By listening to his tender voice telling me to write it down, I saw God accomplish more than I ever dreamed. He brought me peace and healing, along with increased strength. He allowed me to see a glimpse of the story from his perspective, rather than my own. He fulfilled one of the greatest desires of my heart by guiding me to write that book of poems, along with a story to encourage others to keep holding onto Christ through their own valleys of despair.

I knew our published story would end up in Julian's hands, touching him deeply, but a part of me desperately wished for the possibility for Juan David to somehow read it too. At least one of those siblings would know how dearly we loved and fought for all three of them.

I handed my final manuscript over to the publisher in early December of 2011. On December 14, my sweet nephew, Zane Burton, unexpectedly wrote this poem for me, confirming the source of my strength to finally write our story down.

> Strength has known your name,
> And it follows you around.
> Your Strength is keeping you sane,
> You're in God's hands now.
> The support you provide to others
> Is like a river that flows forever.
> You support all, sisters and brothers,
> And leave us all, never.
> Life is tough for us all,
> And it's hard for you, too.
> Summer, winter, spring, or fall
> You still manage to see it all through.
> Thank you for all of your giving,
> Your love and support make life more than worth living.

Strength knew my name. What an incredible reminder from a young teenage boy. I didn't even realize he'd been watching, observing.

It's not what you know; it's who you know. Better yet, it's who knows you. God, my Strength, knew me in the most intimate way, and he knew I needed to share my heart with others in a way I'd never done before.

While I waited for our story to be published, I prepared to teach our next women's Bible study at my local church. We were about to embark on a journey together through Henry Blackaby's study, *Experiencing God.*[1] I asked God to strengthen my faith and open my eyes to see him accomplish things only he could do.

My eyes hadn't even begun to see him yet. When you let God consume you, he takes you places you never thought you could go.

4

TO SEEK GOD FIRST

"Let the morning bring me word of your unfailing love, for I have
put my trust in you. Show me the way I should go,
for to you I lift up my soul."
Psalm 143:8

Rise, My Child

As the sun arises and opens my eyes,
I hear your voice quietly say, "Rise."

Rise, my child, as the dawn doth break,
How I long for you to wake.

Rise, my child, come sit with me.
Open your eyes to my artistry.

Come watch the sun as it rises in the East.
Open my Word for your morning feast.

How I long to start the morning with you,
While the grass still lies covered with dew.

Rise, my child, our time ticks away.
The longer you slumber, the less time to pray.

Rise, my child, seek me first in the morn,
I've visited your days even before you were born.

I know the path laid out for you.
I can help you make choices you'll never rue.

Rise, my child, come seek wisdom for today.
Our time passes quickly while on your bed you still lay.

Rise, my child, though your body screams for rest.
Rest in my arms, Child, and you will be blessed.

Though the clock may say you need one hour more.
I'll give you strength to make you soar.

Rise, my child, you've everything to gain.
The strength you fear losing, my strength will sustain.

Rise, my child, I long for you.
Only my sunrise provides this incredible view!

God always uses the mountains to speak to me. I spent my last summer before graduating from college working as a summer missionary in a tiny Mexican town called Tasquillo, set in the middle of the valley surrounded by mountains all around. I woke up every morning to the breathtaking view of the majestic mountains, but I stood in awe of the view I took in each time we returned from town to begin our descent back down the mountain.

One specific location on the side of the mountain gave a glimpse of the entire little town where we lived. Everything looked so tiny, like miniature doll houses littering the valley below. Even as a young college student, I let God impress the view on my heart so firmly I can still see it today. He reminded me every time I looked over that mountain that he held the whole world in his hands.

He carried all of my daily concerns, which seemed huge at the time, as well as those of millions of other people. That summer, he taught me how big he is. I hoped to capture a snapshot of the view, but I never found the chance to do so. However, if I close my eyes, I can see it again as clearly as if I still stood there.

Thirteen years later, I found myself looking down over a mountain in Bogotá, Colombia. This mountain was higher yet, and the city below so much bigger than that little Mexican town. Seven million people populated this city. Needless to say, the impact of knowing God carried all of us and our daily concerns in his hand was even greater.

He impressed this visual reminder deeply upon my heart, a lesson I would need to hold onto during those times when my daily concerns overwhelmed me. He knew the problems that awaited me. He saw my future. He knew the choices I would make and where they would lead me. He saw the road ahead and knew how to steer me in the right direction. He taught me to seek him and him alone, and he also taught me the need to do so first thing in the morning, before anything else competed for my time and attention. I learned to sit and be still in his presence before each day even begins.

Many changes came with adopting this tranquil hour with God each day. I set my alarm an hour earlier and forced myself out of bed long before any other signs of life appeared in the house. I learned to get ready for work more quickly without focusing so much time on my physical appearance. I rearranged my lifestyle to get to bed at a decent time.

Of course I still grumble my way out of bed or completely ignore the alarm on various occasions. But I soon found myself looking forward to that quiet hour, craving it. I cheated myself when I missed it, and I knew it.

God "wooed" me out of my bed each day, longing to spend time with me. I finally found what many describe as "falling in love with Jesus." It felt amazing, and I'll never be the same again. Never. Once you've tasted such intimacy, I don't know how you can ever be satisfied again without it. Life completely changed, and so did I.

I grew up a perfectionist and a "natural" worrier. I planned my life away and tried to control every last detail. Yet God finally got it through my head that he holds the reins, not me. Fretting and worrying got me nowhere. Planning out my life only wasted precious time I should have used to seek him. How many dead ends could I have avoided by learning this earlier? How many blessings did I miss?

When I need guidance or direction, it comes *after* I seek him *first*. If I need to take the next step, he often gives me the obvious answer *after* I devote my time to him rather than the question at hand. The more in tune I become with his Spirit, the more in tune I become with his daily guidance, direction, and purpose. My heart opened to what he wanted to show and teach me each day rather than what I thought I needed to accomplish. My constant worries seemed to evaporate, and I soon lived with so much peace. When I let go of my quest for control, I found freedom.

Freedom to live each day without needing to manipulate the outcome. To be patient enough to wait for God's timing, which is always better than my own. To trust rather than figure out how to do things myself. To accept what can't be changed and still move on. To see annoying interruptions in life as divine interventions, leading me where I never would have gone or keeping me from going where I wasn't meant to go. To drop my plans when God made it clear he led in a different direction. To let go when things didn't go my way. To accept and actually admit I made a mistake. To enjoy the life God gave me without feeling the need to measure up to someone else. To be honest with the world around me about who I am inside.

I wish I hadn't wasted so much of my life before finding such freedom.

My book came out in February of 2012, four months before our return to Colombia. Yet that month held more than we bargained for, challenging us to hold even more firmly to the faith and freedom we claimed.

Julian officially exited the orphanage in mid-February with no job and nowhere to go. His social worker gave him plenty of warning, plenty of time to find a job and look for a place. I assumed his support team (social worker, psychologist, and defender) would mentor him through the process, helping him secure a job and an apartment before sending him out onto the street, but that didn't happen. Nearly nineteen years old, they now expected him to step up and take responsibility for his life.

I feared the places a lack of money might force him to live. I feared losing contact with him, and I feared what the world might do to this fragile "child." He panicked, and so did I.

Then I heard that still, small voice gently whispering those two familiar words in my ear again.

"Seek me."

All the whirling, anxious activity came to a screeching halt. I knew I had no choice but to obey. God wanted me to stop searching for answers, to seek only him. In all my frantic anxiety, I lost focus of life's purpose.

I reminded myself to be still in his presence. I once again welcomed that hour of quiet with God in the mornings. So why was

I so surprised when God revealed a new direction for Julian during one of those quiet mornings?

I remembered meeting someone in Colombia who had connections with missionaries all over Bogotá. God prompted me one morning to contact her about Julian's situation, to see if she knew of a safe, affordable place for him to live.

"I may have a solution for you. I know a lady here who lives alone but has an extra room available. She is struggling with some health issues and may need a little extra help around the house. She used to teach music in the United States before she retired and moved here."

Within only a day or so, the lady and I spoke with one another about Julian's predicament.

"I really could use some help around here in addition to the rent. However, I'll be moving to another part of Colombia in August, so I can only offer him a place to stay for the next six months." This at least bought him some time to ease into the transition of independent living.

Not only did Julian have a place to go where he could still maintain contact with us, but he also stayed connected to our own network of believers, keeping him surrounded by many who shared our faith. His scenario could have turned out so differently, but by God's grace, it didn't.

As if walking Julian through the exit process wasn't a big enough burden to carry while living on another continent, another piece of news left us speechless. Both Julian and one of the previous house parents from the orphanage recently hinted that things weren't going well for Juan David with his new "family." He spent the last three months with them during his break between school years, expecting to return to the orphanage in early February when the new school year started again. Then he'd continue to spend weekends and holidays with them, just as he'd done for the last year and a half.

Yet when the family returned him to the orphanage to start school again, one of the directors privately shared with Julian that his brother was back for good. No more weekend or holiday breaks awaited him. His second opportunity for a family now fell through.

No. It couldn't be.

I finally accepted another family would soon claim Juan David as their son. Now this? Bewildered, I didn't know what to think or feel about the news.

"God, didn't you tell me to let him go?" I asked with such confusion.

I'd always wondered how that boy dealt with losing us when his hopes to join our family crumbled beneath his feet. Who told him? What did they tell him? How did he react? Who comforted him in the days and weeks that followed? Shortly after coming home from Colombia nearly two years later, Julian put me in touch with the one person able to give me all those answers.

I still remembered her voice from all the times she answered the phone when I called his house. I could almost hear it as I read the words she typed to me, spilling the answers to all of those questions without my even asking. In the moment, I wondered why God continued to fill in those gaps for me. Why did he want me to know?

Through that one contact with his previous house parent, I finally knew the intense heartache Juan David went through when he lost us. He cried for weeks on end, tearfully praying every single night, "God, please bring my Mama Rachelle back to me."

I sighed heavily as I recalled that conversation. I wondered if he felt the same now, losing a second family, a second opportunity. This time he found himself all alone, with his sister long gone, and now his brother, too. My heart suddenly ached for that child I once loved so dearly, believing he was my own. I accepted our loss when I knew another family embraced him. But how could I accept knowing a family no longer claimed him after all?

"If you had another chance to adopt my brother, would you do it?" Julian's words spoken to me months earlier in the summer now rang loudly in my ear.

"Of course we would! But he has a family who loves him now. He's happy, and I want it to work out for him. Besides, Colombia will never give us another chance. They already said no. Twice." I knew we legally couldn't honor our words to try again, but I wondered now if someone in the orphanage might let us at least play a part in Juan David's life.

No family claimed him, and our relationship with Julian should be enough to prove our commitment. Maybe, just maybe, this story was about to come full circle to lead us back to him in some way.

I now prayed earnestly for God to somehow reunite us with this child we once loved as our own.

Thus began the wait to see what God still planned for our beloved Juan David.

5

JULIAN'S ONE DESIRE

"I know your deeds. See, I have placed before you an open door that no one can shut. I know that you have little strength, yet you have kept my word and have not denied my name."
Revelation 3:8

Should We Try Once More?

The door already shut
It practically slammed in our face
We let go and moved on
They showed us no grace.

They never got to meet us
Never saw their mistake.

Nor did they consider how greatly
Their decision made his heart break.

We never failed to love him
As the years kept passing by
Even when a new family embraced him
We grieved never having said good-bye

Yet here we are again
With the possibility in store
He remains an orphan still
Should we try once more?

Before it's too late and no time remains
Before his chances completely run out
Could this door really be open again?
Who am I to doubt?

Continue to reveal yourself
Continue to guide our every thought
We trust fully in your mighty plan
For this child for whom we've fought.

"Let them go. Trust me to take care of them." There was no mistaking his voice nearly six months after the adoption failed, smack dab in the middle of our grief.

With time, we did. We let go. We accepted it, whether we understood it or not. They were not our children, nor would they ever be.

God gave me peace about them. I knew Viviana ended up with the family he'd chosen for her. I trusted Juan David's future looked bright, filled with many opportunities with the family now in the process to adopt him. My heart did not ache for either one of them anymore.

Yet here we were again, heartbroken for Juan David. For some reason, God wouldn't allow me to let go of that boy.

The last I'd heard, he lived with a local family on the week-ends and vacation days and resided at the orphanage on school nights. When he finished the sixth grade back in November, the family took him with them to a beautiful island in Colombia for part of his three-month break from school between November and February. He had no contact with Julian whenever he resided with them. We assumed they planned to adopt him since they treated him like a son.

In fact, we all assumed Juan David's adoption was nearly complete. But his "family" returned him to the orphanage right in time for school to start again in February, never to come back for him. His path crossed with his brother for a few days before Julian aged out of the orphanage. At least they visited with each other one last time before Julian left, giving them a chance to say good-bye.

Our hearts broke when Juan David moved straight into the house with the older boys rather than the house he lived in for so long. Not only did he lose a family again, but he didn't even return to familiar surroundings.

Plus we knew from Julian's experience there that this partic-ular house offered very little love in comparison to the other one. Instead, a colder environment greeted him, one with more behavior problems and stricter rules. I trusted God to take care of him, yet I sat bewildered, wondering how life turned out so unfair.

I honestly didn't know how to take this news. Julian was convinced it meant only one thing. He never stopped believing his brother belonged with us, to us, as our son. He wanted nothing more than to see that become a reality, somehow.

We already planned to arrive in Colombia again within four months' time. Mike gained clearance from his job to stay the entire month of June with Julian. We agreed to volunteer for summer school at the Christian school we visited the year before, so we lined up the dates and purchased our airline tickets.

Our summer plans included both mission work and family time with Julian. Our church approved our travel as an actual mission trip since we'd be volunteering at a Christian school, so our more than generous class at church helped quite a bit with the expenses. That freed up our own funds to continue to help Julian in his transition to independent living.

Nearly a year slipped by already. I missed Julian so much and couldn't wait to hug that boy again. He longed to see us, to finally be surrounded by his family. Yet our attention and anticipation shifted gears, and Juan David took center stage again. I boldly prayed for God to finally reunite us this time, and Julian worked behind the scenes to make that meeting possible.

As I prayed, I recalled the answers God already gave me when I prayed so boldly for this child. The first time I thought I finally let him go, I soon found out about the split between him and his sister. Suddenly my heart ached to know he was okay. I boldly asked God to let me hear from Juan David again someday. Only days later, Julian told me his brother wrote me a letter after eight months of silence to tell me he was happy with a new family.

A year later, right before we left to go to Colombia the first time, I boldly asked God to let us see Juan David again. We did not get to see him during our stay, but Julian arranged a secret video phone call shortly after we arrived back home, giving us all the chance to "see" and talk to Juan David again. Realizing how personally God answered my first two bold prayers, I soon found myself praying daily that God would do more than reunite us.

"God, please give him back to us."

In those four months while we waited to return to Colombia, Julian really struggled to find his personal identity in the world.

Thankfully, God connected him with the right people. He randomly met a neighbor who invited him to a weekly prayer group. He didn't realize it, but he began to build his own little network of other believers in that group who embraced him and looked out for him.

One of the women even met with him on a weekly basis to teach him more about the Bible, to disciple him, and help him grow more in his faith. He formed a beautiful bond with her, giving him one more godly influence in his life, one more person to look to for guidance and support. I really hoped for the chance to meet her and thank her personally for what she'd done for my son spiritually. I prayed for God to meet his spiritual needs in addition to his physical needs, and we watched Him answer those prayers.

One day while I sat at my kitchen table "talking" to Julian on my little pink laptop, he told me all about a lady who took him to church as a child. He'd mentioned her before, but now he suddenly felt a need to tell me so much more about her.

"She used to take us to church with her every week, and she taught us about the Bible. We spent a lot of time at her house. When I was little, I couldn't read very well, and she always helped me with my homework. She taught me how to read and write, and she talked to my teachers whenever my mom couldn't go to the parent conferences. She was like a mom to me. After they put me in the orphanage, she even visited us there one time." She obviously left a lasting impression on him because he still recalled everything she'd done for him, now nearly ten years later.

My heart burned with a desire to meet this woman and thank her for planting those seeds, for the impact she made on him. His spiritual journey began with her, and I knew it would bless her to know the growth that came from the seeds she planted in that child. I wondered if we could find her.

"What is her name? Maybe we could come try and look for her."

"I only remember her first name, Mercedes. Plus I heard a while back that she moved to the United States." With only a first name to go on, our hope of finding her quickly dismissed itself.

Accepting we had no way to find her, I silently prayed for God to bless her abundantly for all she did for those children, specifically him.

Before we knew it, only a few weeks remained until our return to Colombia. We thought we'd already made all the necessary arrangements, but God still had quite a bit more to arrange before we left. He held the reins and followed an agenda we knew nothing about.

While I continued to pray for a reunion with Juan David, Julian worked hard to make that happen. He ran the idea by the orphanage director, and she didn't see any problem with him spending time with us or even staying with us.

I needed to write an official request to obtain formal permission, like I did the year before in order to see Julian. However, that wasn't enough for Julian. He was determined to find a way for us to pursue his brother's adoption a second time. He begged us to try again.

"Impossible. Too much stands against us. It's too late." I argued my case with Julian, yet I knew deep in my heart God may be up to something bigger than I could fathom.

Reality screamed in my face. Too many factors stood in the way. Our first attempt took more than a year. At the time, a false piece of information led us to believe Juan David would turn sixteen in less than six months, making it legally impossible to adopt him internationally. Based on our previous experience, we saw no way to complete the adoption process in time before his sixteenth birthday.

But God suddenly triggered my memory, reminding me of a guy we met in Austin back in 2009 who adopted three siblings from Colombia, one over the age of sixteen. I knew something in the law changed in order to make the older sibling's adoption even possible. I only remembered the guy's first name, Scott, but I knew we needed to contact him to find out more.

I researched Scott's adoption story via the organization we met him through and found a way to contact him. I e-mailed him to explain our situation. I only wanted to know what changed in the law to make his last son's adoption possible.

I still did not believe even a remote possibility existed to try again to adopt Juan David. Honestly, I wanted to hear we didn't have enough time so I could drop it altogether. Knowing we'd likely spend time with him again soon was more than enough for me. If we could play a role in his life again, I'd be happy. We had no desire to face the overwhelming adoption process again.

I didn't really expect to hear back from Scott, so his quick response surprised me. He told us the change in the law wouldn't help us with Juan David at all.

"If you can get them to reopen your case, quickly, I do think there's still enough time to adopt him." Since he'd already adopted from Colombia three different times, I trusted his insight.

"We will be there in just a few weeks. I guess I can put a bug in someone's ear about our continued desire to adopt him." Yes, I admit to my naivety.

"You've got to do more than put a bug in someone's ear. You need to contact a lawyer as soon as possible so he can look into the possibilities before you even get there." Scott probably had no idea how clueless I felt on the other end. Me? Find a lawyer in Colombia? I wouldn't even know where to start.

If I did as he suggested and things actually worked out in our favor to reopen our case, the part of the law that changed might enable us to adopt Julian, too! It would give him the opportunity to immigrate to the United States with his brother, and then we could adopt him here as an adult. That's how Scott adopted his oldest child.

To do so, however, might be a race against time.

We'd been told all along that Julian's chance to be adopted internationally had already passed. He recently celebrated his nineteenth birthday. Yet according to Scott, a sliver of hope still existed. A very short window of opportunity remained for him if we secured the approval to adopt his younger sibling.

He sent me a website that explained things in detail, but it also showed me we only had until November 30 to be cleared through Immigration. It was already May. November suddenly held great significance on our calendar.

Wow. Our minds started spinning. Could this possibility really exist? Did God turn our world upside down all over again? Might he give us another chance and open doors we were told could never open? For *both* of them?

The logistics of it all kept me doubting enough time remained, but my growing relationship with God told me nothing can stop his plans. Sometimes he puts a God-sized task in front of us to prove it is something only he can do. I taught that every week in our Bible study, *Experiencing God*, but did I believe it?

In order to attempt this, we needed to get in contact with a Colombian lawyer as soon as possible to at least find out if the Adoption Committee would even consider reopening our case to adopt Juan David. That sounded complicated enough, so complicated I would normally never follow through. I didn't even have a clue where to start to find a lawyer in Colombia.

Here's where God showed me how incredibly involved he is in every detail of our lives. Not long after Julian exited the orphanage, the lady he lived with shared his story and connection to us with a neighbor family who'd adopted three siblings, one the age of an adult. Our relationship to Julian interested them, so they gave her their lawyer's name and number to pass on to me. They assured her their lawyer could help us adopt Julian. I knew enough about US immigration laws to know we couldn't adopt a nineteen-year-old, so I never responded or contacted the lawyer.

When Scott told me I needed to find a lawyer quickly, I mentioned that someone recently gave me the name of one in Bogotá.

"I know several attorneys there. Do you mind me asking what name they gave you?"

You can imagine my surprise when he told me that, out of all the attorneys in Bogotá, he used the very same one for his second adoption! The world just got quite a bit smaller.

"He's probably one of the best adoption lawyers in Bogotá. I could not have been any more pleased to work with him. I'll even call him first to give him a heads up about your situation." This stranger had a huge heart for adoption and seemed so eager to help us.

Now we had no choice but to follow through. God knew I would drag my feet way too long, so he literally pushed us right into action.

Two days later, I contacted the lawyer personally to give him our case number and information, and he started making phone calls and visits to everyone involved in our case. We barely even had a chance to think about it before God set this whole thing into motion.

6

A DIVINE APPOINTMENT

"Call to me and I will answer you and tell you great and
unsearchable things you do not know."
Jeremiah 33:3

A Lamb in the Shepherd's Arms

When darkness surrounds you,
And light can't be seen,
When questions overwhelm you,
And life seems so mean,

Your hopes seem to shatter,
Your faith crumbles at your feet.

Your strength is stolen from you,
You can barely stand the heat.

You've reached the point of no return,
But with complete surrender you rest
As a lamb in the Shepherd's arms,
Lay your head upon his chest.

Allow him to carry you
To where you've never gone before.
He'll turn your weakness into strength
And give you wings to make you soar.

Heights you've never imagined
Wait for your eyes to see.
When your heart beats in tune with the Shepherd's
You become all he's prepared you to be.

Tuesday, June 5, 2012, arrived very quickly. Luggage in hand, we were about to embark on our second journey to Colombia. My, oh, my, how things changed, pretty much overnight.

God prepared to lift us to a whole new height to watch even more of his plan unfold before our eyes. Now thirty days lay before us, jam-packed with more activity than we ever imagined. Our previous fifteen carefree days the year before would not even compare to the thirty ahead of us. Carefree would not fit into our vocabulary this time around.

We stayed in a pretty tiny apartment the previous year, but it provided everything we needed. The space in our current apartment pleasantly surprised us, especially since it was located in the same complex. Two floors, with a bedroom on the first floor and two bedrooms upstairs. Two bathrooms. A small kitchen. A laundry room (separate from the kitchen this time). A living/dining area. An office.

I even hoped for a small patio area to sit outside in the mornings with my cup of coffee, and God granted me that wish as well. In addition to all the extra room, several closets offered even more space, plus we found a TV screen and DVD player, a working phone, and a modem for the internet. We felt so blessed.

Mike and I took the bedroom upstairs with the biggest bed. Julian wanted the bedroom downstairs that could be closed off with his bathroom to give him more privacy. We bought a sleeping bag for David since the extra bedroom had no bed. But another teacher from the Christian school who lived in the same apartment complex let us borrow a mattress for him to use, which actually turned out to be the most comfortable bed of all.

The coordinator of the English Institute for the school, Zayde, came over to meet us our first morning.

"It's so good to meet you! I wanted to let you know that we are having a summer school meeting on Friday at the coffee shop inside the mall. It will be a good chance for you to meet the rest of the team that you'll be working with." Her bubbly personality immediately drew us to her. She had a daughter close in age to David, so we found some common ground right away.

"I also would like to know if you can join us for church on Sunday?" She offered to let us ride along with her family to the local Baptist church.

I looked at Julian, knowing he wanted to take us to the church he attended.

"That's fine. We can go with them this week, and then we'll go to my church the next week," Julian said.

Later that morning, we took an entire suitcase of things over to the house where Julian lived. The lady he lived with had been a music teacher in the United States, but she decided to take some time to travel and live abroad after she retired. She kindly asked us if we could possibly bring her a few things on her wish list, things either not available in Colombia or incredibly expensive there.

Our friends from church all chipped in and bought her almost every single thing on her list. We needed to take an extra suitcase because we had so much extra stuff. God not only blessed her through our class by giving generously to her, but he went above and beyond to bless her even more when the airline waived the fee for the extra suitcase.

"It's like Christmas in June!" Her eyes lit up as she rummaged through the suitcase of all the goodies she missed while living in Colombia. She took Julian in as a stranger when he had nowhere to go, and God blessed her for it.

My heart melted when we walked into Julian's bedroom. All those pictures I'd tearfully taken down from our walls at home now hung right above his bed. The little white bear and stuffed duck, tangible reminders of his sister, lay on his bed, right on top of his pillow. He loved his siblings and obviously missed them incredibly.

This lady planned to move at the end of the summer, so she expressed concern over where Julian might live after she left. She talked with several people about his need, but no one responded. We assured her we'd continue to look into more possibilities while we were there, but a gut feeling told me the person meant to take him in hadn't even entered the picture yet.

The next morning, I called our lawyer to let him know we finally arrived in Colombia. We ate breakfast at the mall, so I called him from the outdoor eating area on the top floor, looking straight at the mountains all around us.

"Bienvenidos a Colombia!" He warmly welcomed us to his country. His caring voice put me right at ease. "Listen, I have good news. The Family Welfare Office agreed to at least meet with you. They haven't given me any available dates yet, but I will contact you as soon as I hear anything more from them. I am so eager to finally meet you in person."

A date would have been nice, but at least they were open to hear us out.

Later that day, we met the summer school crew, or at least most of them, at the local coffee shop inside the mall. It felt good to finally connect and meet the people we'd work with every day. We hung out for a while to get to know each other and discussed the overall plans for summer school.

Julian did not join us that morning because he attended a weekly course on Fridays to prepare him for the workforce. He enjoyed the classes, and they really boosted his sense of self. He returned home right at sunset, and then he and I grabbed a taxi to head to his weekly prayer meeting. Mike and David opted out due to the language barrier.

It blessed me to finally meet the people Julian met and prayed with each week. Recalling the way God connected him to the group still brings me goose bumps.

Desperate to secure a place to live before the day he had to leave the orphanage, he took a bus to the house to meet the lady he now lived with. When no one answered the door, a neighbor started talking to him. She invited him in to her home for coffee and ended up sharing her testimony with him. He found out she attended the same church he went to as a child, and she invited him to go with her. She later invited him into this intimate group of believers and even discipled him for a while.

God answered my prayers for Julian to build a spiritual support network by connecting him with this little group. They embraced me that night as much as I cherished the opportunity to meet all of them. They even asked me to lead the devotion the next week, and they asked Julian to choose the music for the evening.

I had never led a Bible study in Spanish before, so my mind immediately raced with questions over whether I even had the ability.

Yet God already prepared me with a book he conveniently nudged me to pack in my suitcase.

Julian worked with a group of younger kids from his orphanage every Saturday, so he left pretty early the next morning. He still hadn't found a job, and this was his only way of making any money. He made very little, but he enjoyed it, and it gave him something to do and take pride in.

While Julian worked on Saturdays, Mike, David, and I found some fun things to do. We returned to the infamous go-karts we'd found the year before, and we ate waffles and ice cream at our favorite restaurant. We requested to spend the day with Juan David that first Saturday, but the right people hadn't responded yet, so we couldn't take him out after all. Maybe the following weekend might work out better.

Our new friend Zayde picked us up early on Sunday morning to take us to church with her family, along with another summer teacher who'd just arrived from Montana. A missionary from Canada translated the service for Mike and David, and I really enjoyed seeing Julian use that little Bible we'd sent him the year before.

"Don't forget. Tomorrow is the cookout at our sister church to help them raise the needed funds to complete the second floor in their building." I tuned out most of the announcements before the service, but for some reason I remembered hearing that one.

On the way home, Zayde asked if we'd like to accompany her family to the cookout. Since we didn't have any kind of schedule yet, we readily agreed. We never could have known why God arranged for us to attend that cookout the next day. One of the most divine encounters of our entire summer awaited us, only a few days into our journey.

Once we arrived at the cookout, Zayde quickly showed us around the little Baptist church.

"Why don't you walk around all the tables to see what you want to eat? Each table offers a typical Colombian dish. We've already paid for your meals." Zayde left us alone for a few minutes while we browsed the different food choices. Everything looked so unfamiliar.

Julian developed a strange attitude as soon as we arrived that began to irritate me. We sadly already witnessed his horrible eating habits, refusing to eat much of anything besides dessert (one of the many effects of being raised in an institution).

"Choose something to eat, Julian. Someone already paid for your meal." I spoke to him firmly on the matter.

"I really don't want anything. My stomach is hurting right now. I just don't want to be here. This place gives me bad vibes. I used to go to school close by when I was young, and I don't like being anywhere near here."

Julian continued to whine and pleaded for us to leave. Little did I know how strongly the powers of darkness worked against us that day. Unbeknownst to us, a miracle hovered around that cookout.

I ignored Julian's pleas to leave and continued to look around, trying to choose what I wanted to eat and help David find something he might actually like (also a very picky eater, but understandable when he's not in his own country).

I turned around for a brief second to find Julian hugging someone. His whole mood suddenly changed as a huge smile quickly spread across his face.

"Who is this?" I asked awkwardly.

"This is Mercedes." The smile on his face spoke volumes. Tears of joy threatened to spill down my cheeks. The very woman we thought we could never find because we only knew her first name.

Years passed since he'd seen her, but he recognized her immediately. I stood there in absolute awe.

"Julian told me so much about you. I always wanted to meet you so I could thank you for everything you did for him as a child." I could hardly believe God had just given me the chance to meet her and thank her. I treasure the picture we took of the three of us together on that unforgettable day.

"Julian with his two moms." She barely even knew me, but her comment showed the deep connection we immediately shared.

I embraced the opportunity to personally tell her how far he'd come spiritually from the seeds she planted so long ago. She responded with the verse about our different spiritual roles, where one man plants and another man waters. She knew the Word inside and out, reciting Scripture continually while we talked.

Here we acted as partners in a work God began in Julian since he was a small child, and now he divinely brought us together as partners in his future. He reached a stage where he needed both of us, one in much closer proximity than the other. Truthfully, God would use her in more ways than we ever imagined at the time.

We explained our failed attempt to adopt his siblings and let her know Viviana moved to Europe with her new adoptive mother. It saddened her to hear they separated the kids. She loved all three of those children more dearly than I knew.

"But Juan David is back in the orphanage again, and we contacted a lawyer to inquire if our case can be reopened to still adopt him." What a blessing to talk about those kids to a "stranger" who loved them, too.

"Juan David. Mi alma!" She spoke so tenderly about that boy, recalling his genuine faith as a child. Her eyes lit up when I mentioned his name, showing me he was worth the fight.

We gained an amazing prayer warrior when we met her, with a beautiful connection to those kids. All three of them. She even involved her whole church to pray Juan David home to us.

In a city of seven million people, only God arranges "random" meetings like this.

We call it a divine appointment.

In Colombia they call it a "Diosidencia" (a God-coincidence).

I call it amazing.

7

BRINGING THE BOX DOWN

"The LORD your God, who is going before you, will fight for you."
Deuteronomy 1:30

A Second Chance?

You set us on a journey
Saying only, "Follow me."
We knew not where it headed
Yet we followed obediently.

You led us from a mountaintop
Down to a valley of despair.
You let us struggle through our faith
And wonder why you didn't care.

You lifted us from the pit,
Out of the darkness in which we lived.
You gave us hope to stand again,
And light after we grieved.

The sadness we somehow survived
Became a story of grace for all to read.
You took us back up to the mountain
After we surrendered the lead.

But our journey didn't stop there,
As we continued to seek your face.
You ordered each step before us,
Leading us through every phase.

Our journey now leads us to
Another leap of faith in the dark.
I suspect you'll be there to catch us
And place us right on the mark.

A week and a half passed in Colombia by the time we heard from our lawyer again. He called me while I was teaching a class, so I returned his call when we took a short break.

"The Family Welfare Office set a specific time to review your case next week, but they still haven't agreed on the exact day they can meet with you. What is your schedule like at the school?"

"I teach a class until noon every day, but we are free any time after that."

"Okay. That's good. Keep yourselves available at 3:00 in the afternoon for both Wednesday and Thursday." He seemed eager to get this meeting scheduled for us.

Simple enough, right? Maybe. Until you consider again the spiritual warfare we faced in trying to make that meeting happen.

We begged for this opportunity nearly three years ago while trying to appeal our case. I always wondered if it might have made a difference to meet us in person rather than read about us on paper. We finally had the chance to find out.

I can't say we were the same people anymore. We grew and changed through that experience. I felt conflicted, a part of me nervous while the other part of me felt incredible peace and confidence. I knew God opened this door. He would speak through us.

For us.

Actually, He already went ahead of us to prepare the way.

That night Julian and I went to his weekly prayer meeting at his neighbor's house. I prepared a devotion based on lessons I'd gleaned through reading a Spanish translation of Priscilla Shirer's book, *Interrupción Divina (Life Interrupted)*[2] while on the plane. I thanked God for convincing me to pack that book at the last minute.

Julian's bus arrived much later than expected because of traffic, so he didn't even walk into the apartment until 7:00 p.m., the time we needed to arrive at the prayer meeting. We made him a quick sandwich before he and I rushed back out the door to grab a taxi.

"We thought maybe you weren't coming!" Relief was written all over his friends' faces when we finally walked through the door.

After spending some time praying and singing the songs Julian picked out, they gave me the floor to share. I embraced the opportunity to share the message God laid on my heart.

"Facing problems of any kind or magnitude leaves us with two choices. We can complain about our plans getting interrupted or we can see them as divine, leading us to something even greater than our plans." I had them read several related scriptures and asked questions about what they knew about certain people in the Bible who made the better choice.

I ended by sharing my testimony of our "failed adoption."

"What seemed to be the hardest tragedy in our life actually turned into one of the greatest blessings ever because it led us to Colombia and to Julian. Now it might even lead us back to Juan David." My eyes locked with Julian's tear-filled eyes. Not a single eye remained dry by the time I finished.

I cherished the opportunity to not only meet this special group of people from Julian's life and encourage them through their own challenges, but also to share our story and our testimony with them. God used me to give the orphan a voice, despite the fact that Julian sat week after week with these people. They embraced him in a new way after that night, plus they joined our army of prayer warriors to pray for Juan David's adoption.

We stayed busy at the school every day. We made new friends daily and felt very comfortable there. We'd settled into our apartment, managed to get around easily by public transportation, and we tried several new Colombian dishes served for lunch in the school cafeteria.

Our trip so far seemed positive and rewarding. God already answered numerous prayers from the last year in just the first two weeks.

Once again, we attempted to see Juan David during our second weekend. Sadly, we still waited on an approval from one specific person. His defender. Without that approval, we couldn't have any contact with him.

It happened to be Father's Day weekend, so Julian looked forward to taking us to his church on such a special day. He was able to celebrate the day with Mike, his "dad," for the second year in a row now after growing up without any father figure in his life.

Mike woke up on Saturday morning with an ache in his tooth that hurt even worse as the day went on. It gave him quite a headache as well. We were determined to spend a fun day together, but the intensity of Mike's toothache dampened the mood significantly.

When he woke up on Sunday morning, he could barely stand it anymore. He agreed to go to church with us, but you could tell he really wanted to stay in bed and sleep to avoid the increasing pain.

Julian noticed the tension in Mike's face all morning and wondered what put him in such a bad mood, but David and I knew he had to hurt pretty badly because he normally had a very high tolerance to pain. The normal, over-the-counter pain medications weren't cutting it.

By the time the church service ended, we ditched our plans to take Mike out for lunch and caught a taxi instead to head straight home. We purchased an antibiotic over the counter at the pharmacy by the apartment, hoping it would help alleviate an obvious infection.

"This is the most intense pain I've ever experienced in my entire life!" Mike laid in the recliner, moaning and groaning, all day.

We called our friend Zayde to see if she could help us find a dentist. Before we knew it, four or five different people from the Christian school tried to connect us with one. What an incredible support system that school provides for their teachers coming from abroad!

The fact it was Sunday complicated the matter since most dentists wouldn't see patients on the weekend. Then Monday happened to be a holiday, so we couldn't find help for him until Tuesday. Meanwhile, Mike begged to see someone immediately. I never in my life saw him react that way!

David and I knew it was bad because Mike hates being an inconvenience to others. Thankfully, the antibiotic finally kicked in by early evening, the pain became bearable, and he said he could wait until Tuesday. We thanked God for being able to purchase an antibiotic so easily.

One of my summer student's mothers worked as a dental hygienist, so she agreed to look at Mike's tooth right there at the school on Tuesday morning. After a quick look, she explained what she saw and what options existed to treat it. She said the best decision would be to completely extract the tooth, offering to schedule him the following afternoon if he chose that route. After Mike got his own dentist's agreement, he scheduled the procedure as soon as possible.

But the Family Welfare Office still hadn't set a day for our meeting, so we couldn't commit for the dental appointment. Things definitely grew complicated, which isn't fun when you're out of the country and out of your comfort zone.

Thankfully, our lawyer called me that afternoon to confirm our meeting time for Thursday afternoon at three o'clock. We quickly made arrangements for the dental appointment on Wednesday afternoon so he wasn't still in pain for our meeting on Thursday. I wondered how much pain might still linger after the procedure, and I hoped and prayed it didn't affect how we presented ourselves at the meeting.

We waited far too long for this opportunity, and we only had one shot to prove ourselves.

After a complicated morning on Wednesday, we took a taxi into town to meet the dental hygienist outside of her office building. She walked us to one building to get X-rays and then led us to her office for the procedure. I took comfort in the fact that I taught her young son in my class that summer, so we already connected. She treated my husband with the same respect that I treated her little boy.

David and the little boy played a quiet game together in the corner of the office while I attempted to translate between the dentist and Mike (wish I would have brushed up on my dental vocabulary). I thanked God for the gorgeous view of the mountains from the office window. It helped to calm my own nerves throughout the whole procedure.

Mike did well, and before we knew it, the dentist stitched him up. She went over all the instructions with me regarding the medications he needed to get at the pharmacy, and then we paid the bill. Mike went straight to bed as soon as we got home to rest and recover.

What a long day, and tomorrow would be even longer. I kept praying Mike would be in good spirits so nothing hindered our meeting at the Family Welfare Office.

Mike stayed home Thursday morning to recover while I headed to school to make an attempt to teach, despite my stomach already tied in knots. Julian found out his social worker planned to be at the meeting, so that at least helped ease our minds a bit. We knew she could help vouch for the familial role we played in Julian's life.

As soon as I got home from school, we bid good-bye to Julian and asked him to pray. Depending on how this meeting went, we might even have the chance to take Juan David with us on a mini-vacation over the weekend. Zayde and her family invited us to join them for a long weekend in a warmer part of the country.

A taxi soon dropped us off, and we stepped out onto the pavement in the very same location where we'd once mailed all of our adoption documents. What a surreal feeling! We finally stood in the place I long gave up hope of ever seeing.

We waited outside for a few minutes until our attorney arrived and introduced himself. I wasn't surprised to find him to be the warm, kind-hearted man I sensed from our phone conversations. He made us all feel very comfortable and immediately started prepping me as we walked into the building.

"What they want to see today is that the three of you are truly united in your adoption desire. They want to know for sure you all want this, that it's not just you." He looked me straight in the eye with those last words.

It made me wonder if maybe that's why they denied our original appeal. Since I'd written everything in the appeal letter, maybe they felt I pushed for the adoption without the full support of my family. Had my voice spoken too loudly? Now we'd at least get our chance to see if meeting us in person would speak louder than a piece of paper.

As I tried to process his comment, our attorney continued to make conversation to get to know us better. He asked about the school we volunteered at.

"That's a Christian school for missionaries, isn't it?"

"Yes," I said, wondering how he knew.

"A friend of mine works there, and we go to church together on Sundays." When he told me the name of the church, I realized the director of the school attended that church, too. I gathered this man was a fellow believer. No wonder he seemed to have a heart of gold. Only God.

He walked us down a hallway and invited us to sit on a small white bench outside the room where we would meet. We continued to talk about random things to make conversation until he introduced us to two men who walked over to us.

As soon as he said their names, it all came flooding back.

I knew those names well. I'd prayed very specifically for them when they reviewed our case and our appeal nearly three years ago. The same two men who made the final decision to deny us in the first place. I prayed so hard for God to change their hearts and open their eyes to see who we really were.

Now we finally walked into that long awaited meeting to plead our case—in person this time. Not a single piece of paper preceded us.

Our case changed considerably over the last three years, and so did we. Yet we remained determined to prove our dedication to one particular boy who still waited for a family. Juan David. We were committed to fight for him.

One of the men spoke English, so they let Mike know he could express himself comfortably in the meeting. They still worried Mike would be too withdrawn and introverted, like our original personality test described him. They also wanted to see I wasn't the only one trying to push this adoption. They especially wanted to know how David felt about it.

Shortly after starting our meeting, both men realized I spoke more Spanish than they spoke English, so they still counted on me to translate the entire interview. Ugh. This didn't seem to tip in our favor. I grasped for words in my limited vocabulary, and I could tell by their reactions that I didn't represent either one of us well. My nerves were shot, so my Spanish came out pretty rusty.

Our lawyer did not have permission to participate verbally in the meeting, except when it came time to talk legally. He supported us with his presence alone. The boys' social worker, who could have represented us well, did not end up coming due to being called elsewhere at that particular time.

Needless to say, the meeting didn't go as smoothly as I preferred. I was a nervous wreck trying to translate for everyone and still keep Mike in the loop throughout the entire interview. Mike couldn't follow the conversation as well as he would have liked because I was too flustered to come up with the best vocabulary at the right times. Several times I found myself so caught up in the conversation with the two men that I even forgot to translate for Mike!

David was so nervous when they talked to him that the tears nearly spilled down his cheeks. Scared to death he might say something wrong, he carried a heavy weight on his shoulders when he tried to answer their questions. Thankfully, they liked David and lightened up with him, but they were not easy on us at all. I felt attacked on many levels.

I felt like someone had beaten me up. Just looking at our complete, unapproved file sitting there on the table was enough to make my head spin, remembering all the time, money, energy, and stress behind each piece of paper. I recalled a period of time during my grieving when I couldn't even bear to look at a single adoption document because it made me hyperventilate.

God still spoke through us, despite my obvious shortcomings. They heard what he wanted them to hear. Our presence spoke volumes because we were all in new territory.

"We don't even know if this is legally possible. You do realize that no one has ever done this before? No one has ever come back two-and-a-half years later to request a case to be reopened that was already closed and returned to the file." They reminded us of the general rule in Colombia, once denied, always denied. They don't let you try again.

We defied the odds and tried again.

Our confidence to come before these men and our willingness to go through the process a second time let them see how united we were as a family, how determined we were in our purpose. By the end of the meeting, we found favor in their eyes.

God did answer that prayer from long ago. He changed their hearts toward us, just like I asked him to. Almost three years later.

They needed to present our case to the Head of Adoptions, and that lady would determine whether or not our case could legally be reopened. The men also wanted to speak separately with both Julian and Juan David. They wanted Julian's side of the story and his impression of us as "parents." They wanted to make sure Juan David even still wanted to be part of our family.

Emotionally exhausted, Mike and I thanked the men for their time and then followed our attorney. He stopped to talk to several people in the building and then walked us out to get a taxi.

"We'll be in touch soon." His eyes held hope as he said good-bye while holding the taxi door open for me.

Since the boys' social worker didn't make it to the meeting, we couldn't even ask about seeing Juan David that weekend. I didn't yet realize how much disappointment that fact carried.

As soon as we slipped in the taxi, I fought tears the entire way home. I know we ended on a positive note with pretty good news. But as defensive as I needed to be throughout the meeting, I felt like I just walked off a battlefield.

I moved on without answers. God gave me peace even if I didn't have them. I didn't need them. Finally the answers sat right across from me at the table. I had the chance to ask anything I ever wanted to, yet I had no desire. I didn't want to go back in time. I no longer needed those answers. I only wanted to keep moving forward.

"Do you know and understand our reasons for not approving this adoption last time?" Their question burned in my mind now.

No, we didn't. We never received any explanation when they denied our appeal. But how did we explain that we didn't need to know? What Satan meant to destroy us, God always meant to use for good.

One of the men opened that old file once again to dig out the letter we never received. He read it aloud to us, but I can't remember a word of it. Not a single word. Why open a wound that already healed? God blocked my ears from hearing it because I didn't need to go back in time. The peace he'd given me was enough. The story turned out exactly as it was always meant to.

Why dig up the past now when only the future mattered?

Still, walking away from the meeting I never thought we'd have completely overwhelmed me. Reflecting over everything said over the last three hours flooded me with more emotions than I could handle all at once.

When you're in the moment, you go through the motions, trying to survive each minute and take in as much as you can. Once it's over and you walk away, the reality of what you experienced actually hits. In addition to all of that, I finally got my hopes up to see Juan David that weekend and take him on our mini-vacation. What a huge disappointment.

Darkness covered the sky by the time we arrived back to the mall across the street from our apartments. We went inside the food court to find something to eat before crossing the bridge back to the apartment.

When we finally walked in the door, Julian greeted us and reached out to give me a hug. As I hugged him in return, I couldn't hold the tears back any longer. I think I cried all night long.

I assumed Mike and David knew how I felt, but the surprised looks on their faces told me they didn't. "Maybe you went to a different meeting than we did," Mike responded almost sarcastically, "because I thought everything ended on a positive note. I don't understand at all why you're crying now." I don't know that I understood either.

I thought back to my grieving experience when we originally "lost" the kids. I'd made a mental decision to stuff it all into a box, put the box up on the shelf, and pretend it wasn't there. I thought I'd already brought the box down and faced the contents when I wrote about our journey to Julian. Yet the most painful contents remained in the box.

I had to bring it back down. Again.

Facing those men. Pleading our case. Staring at our complete "unapproved" file in front of us. Considering the thought of going through the adoption process all over again. If I brought the box down, it meant I had to face the contents all over again, whether I was ready or not.

I was so thankful for a mini-vacation from our vacation that weekend because I sure needed time to rest and recuperate from a hectic week. God knew a huge blessing lurked right around the corner, a beauty you can only experience in the valley.

A family in the school offered a vacation home for us to use. We didn't know how big it was or what arrangements awaited each family, but we knew it was much warmer than Bogotá and it had a pool. Ten of us traveled together: our family including Julian, Zayde's family, and three single missionaries from the States who worked alongside us at the school.

Part Two

BACK TO THE VALLEY...

8

DOUBLY BLESSED

"He makes me lie down in green pastures, he leads me beside
quiet waters, he restores my soul."
Psalm 23:2-3a

I Felt Compelled to Ask

A surrendered heart,
A tearful plea,
So stuck in my misery.
Then I heard a tender whisper,
"Child, give them back to me."

I let them go,
I held them high,

Open hands up to the sky.
He convinced me I could trust him
Even if I never knew why.

Life went on,
Hearts on the mend,
Yet I felt compelled to say,
"If you would do one thing for me,
Let me hear from them someday."

A letter written,
A phone call arranged,
Sweet messages soon danced between us.
Then they whisked her away, left him alone,
Our hearts left again to fuss.

A sister gone,
A brother forced to leave,
Not even a future family in sight.
"I'm all alone," he cried out to me.
So my heart again began to fight.

Life stood still.
How could this be?
I felt compelled to ask boldly.
"Oh, God, if it be your will now,
Would you give him back to me?"

Oh, how little did we expect the amazing blessings God gave us over the following two weekends, gifts to cherish and hold close to our hearts for many years to come. Also, the last two blessings before we descended down the mountain toward the valley below.

Still disappointed about Juan David not joining us on our weekend trip, we tried to look forward to a few days of relaxing in the sun. A warm climate. A pool. Hammocks. It sure sounded inviting! Julian came with us, so at least we got to share the experience with him.

Our three-hour journey down and around the mountain to Apulo began quite early on Saturday morning. We passed a few really nice houses along the way, which made us wonder what this vacation home might look like. Yet as we continued to drive, the road became narrower and dustier, and the homes we passed seemed to grow smaller and smaller.

We now wondered where in the world the road headed. Finally that little dusty road led straight to a beautiful condominium home. Our jaws dropped as we walked through the door of this beautiful hidden paradise, our home for the weekend.

Rather than the "house" we all imagined, we found ourselves in an environment you would find on some exotic island. Several "hut-like" rooms for each family, with private bathrooms. Large, comfortable beds. Huge windows that opened to the gorgeous mountain view all around us. An exotic shower. Relaxing, inviting hammocks on every corner. Palm trees. Coconut trees. Orange trees with fresh, juicy oranges to pick for breakfast. A huge, refreshing pool. A warm jacuzzi. Rich, spicy foods with a cook on staff to make the most scrumptious meals. She cooked breakfast and lunch for us every day, and she served us, as well.

Absolutely amazing. No words or pictures captured the beauty and the atmosphere. A true blessing.

We spent a beautiful weekend together in that little hidden paradise, tucked neatly away in a valley surrounded by mountains on all sides. I would wake up early each morning, the early riser I am, to take a long, quiet walk with God around the golf course right behind our little "cabin." Later I'd fall into a hammock to relax for a while. Once Mike woke up, we would head to the kitchen to start some coffee, or we'd pick an orange right off the tree and share it.

Later we all congregated together in the kitchen for a delicious breakfast, and then the kids got ready to swim for the remainder of the day. We ate lunch again in the early afternoon, cooked and served by the lady who worked in the kitchen, and then we all worked together to make something smaller for dinner later in the evening. Once the sun finally set and the sky grew dark, we stayed outside to admire the huge blanket of stars above us.

We walked around with cameras all day long, though not a single picture truly captured the magnificence of the place. Thankfully the experience is forever ingrained in our memories as a gift we didn't see coming. The warmth and the rest did wonders for our souls.

We arrived during the late morning on Saturday, and we stayed until mid-afternoon on Monday. Even the ride back proved to be another blessing in and of itself. The scenes I tried to take in as we wound our way back up the mountain were indescribable. The most vivid shades of green I'd ever seen. Lush vegetation. Exotic fruits and plants growing all up and down the mountainside. The higher we climbed, the more breathtaking the view became, looking down over the mountains and valleys below us. Colombia held more beauty than I ever knew, and it would forever be a part of me.

But we didn't arrive home as well-rested as we assumed after spending such a relaxing weekend away. You see, the altitude can really affect you if you're not used to it. As that little car kept climbing back up the mountain toward Bogotá, we were getting the wind knocked out of us. I didn't realize how hard it would actually be to wake up the following morning, nor how exhausted I would feel all day. After a long nap the next afternoon, I woke up to our second blessing.

"I've got good news." Julian hung up the phone after talking to his social worker and came out of his room almost singing. "You can see Juan David this weekend!"

A day to celebrate, indeed! We finally gained the legal permission necessary to see him again over our final weekend in Colombia. We still had no idea if our case could be reopened, but at least we'd get to spend some time with him. God answered my bold prayer to reunite us with the child we loved for so long, the child I once assumed we would never see again.

After that, those last three days of summer school turned into a blur for me. Everything, for that matter, turned into a blur. Sometimes you've got so much going on you don't fully experience any of it. You're just there, going through the motions. That's how it began to feel for me.

We had spent an entire month now as a family in another country, in addition to having another young adult family member with us who only spoke Spanish—and who displayed multiple effects of being raised in an institution. Two languages competed for attention, and two cultures battled each other, day in and day out. Thankfully, the school we volunteered in was English-speaking.

We met and bonded with so many new people. We tried new foods every day, while struggling to keep enough food in the refrigerator at home. Life sure did cost a lot more in Colombia, and we started to run out of money after the second week. On top of everything else, we faced the emotional and legal challenge to reopen our adoption case. With so many emotions running wild, it's no wonder we found our hearts incredibly guarded against really feeling any of it.

"They can come to pick Juan David up around 4:00 on Friday afternoon. We will need to talk privately first to discuss what they should expect, as well as what they can and cannot say to him." His social worker spoke frankly over the phone to Julian on Thursday evening, giving him information to pass on to us. We waited for so long to see Juan David again. Part of me felt like it was almost too good to be true.

We brought summer school to a close around noon on Friday, took lots of pictures, and then bid our good-byes to everyone. We arrived home around two o'clock, only to leave again by three o'clock for an hour-long taxi ride to the orphanage.

"I'm sorry. She's not working today. Is there someone else who can help you?" The young girl who worked in the office at the orphanage had no idea the disappointment her words held.

We arrived at the orphanage on time only to find out the social worker wasn't even working that day, and the psychologist was in a meeting because she didn't know what time we were coming. We also found out Juan David was not even there! No one would be available to talk to us until after five o'clock, and Juan David would not be back for at least another hour after that.

Sigh. Of course it was too good to be true.

More obstacles now stood in our way, leaving us no choice but to wait it out. Showing our impatient American side wouldn't do any good or help our case in any way.

The psychologist finally returned from her meeting and invited me into her office to talk.

"You need to keep Juan David grounded while he is with you. Make sure he doesn't come back with lofty dreams in his head that might not come true." She spoke wisely. Nobody knew how this would play out, so we needed to protect his young heart.

Believe me, the last thing we wanted to do was break his heart *again*. I fully guarded my own heart, and I wanted nothing more than to enjoy these few days together without trying to tie it to an unknown future. I learned that lesson the hard way.

She also warned me to keep an eye on my own biological child, to watch how he reacted to everything. Could he even handle an older sibling?

"Let me call his house to see if he arrived home yet."

He was there! Ten minutes later, Mike, David, Julian, and I walked together from the office building over to the very same house where we met and picked up Julian a year ago. But this time we looked for Juan David's face as we walked through the door.

We followed Julian through the front door of the house, and a shorter boy with a head full of curly hair immediately reached out his hand to David.

"Hola, David!" He shook David's hand, but David didn't have any idea who the curly-haired boy even was. He figured it was someone who met him the year before when we came for Julian.

I caught sight of a little mole on the boy's right cheek, and I immediately recognized him. Juan David.

"It's been a long time!" I reached out to hug him.

"Yes, it sure has." He leaned in to my embrace.

After that moment, things felt incredibly awkward. Nobody knew what to say. We helped him with his things and told the lady of the house we'd bring him back on Monday afternoon. Soon all five of us squeezed into a taxi, Juan David squashed against me, David on my lap.

I should have felt elated. Instead, I felt terrified. What if we didn't click anymore? What if he has greater issues and needs now than we can handle? What if David really couldn't handle the change? What if everything Juan David had been exposed to over the past few years would come into our home and attack all of the values we held dear as a family?

In those first few minutes of the taxi ride, I found myself begging God to please close this door before it opened any further. I wanted nothing more than to spend a nice weekend with this child, say the good-bye we never got to say, and then return home to enjoy life again as a little family of three. I held David close to me, hugging and squeezing him tightly, reminding him how dearly

I loved him and cherished him. Needless to say, my heart quickly filled with so many mixed emotions.

The boys talked and joked around the whole way home, with me translating in order to keep David in the conversation. Julian and Juan David enjoyed the reunion as well since they had no contact with one another for several months.

We stopped at the grocery store by the apartment to get something to make for dinner. As we walked out with bags in hand, we noticed a beautiful fireworks show coming from across the street at the mall.

There we stood, with Juan David in between us, watching the magnificent colors light up the entire sky above us.

"They do a show like this at the end of every month to try to get more people to come shop at the mall." Julian explained.

Mike, however, captured the moment perfectly.

"Oh, I thought they were doing a show to celebrate Juan David being with us this weekend!"

We stood there in front of the grocery store—all five of us, holding our bags of food while we watched the rest of the show. A fitting way to begin our weekend, to celebrate a long overdue reunion.

God lit up the whole sky to whisper to me, "Here you go, my child. The answer to your prayer."

9

RECONNECTING

"Forget the former things; do not dwell on the past. See, I am doing a new thing! Now it springs up; do you not perceive it? I am making a way in the desert and streams in the wasteland."

Isaiah 43:19

What Do I Say?

There you stood in front of me
Yet I knew not what to say.
So much time already passed
Since that sad November day.

Two years slipped between us
Along with another family

Yet despite so many changes
Three words still flowed naturally.

I told you that I loved you
While we shared a long embrace.
Yet to hear you say you loved me in return
Twas' indeed a kiss of grace.

Now here we are together
With a single goal in mind.
I cherish this chance to reconnect,
To let the time rewind.

Juan David quickly settled into Julian's bedroom for our first evening
to ever spend together, all five of us. After we ate a light dinner, Mike
made some popcorn for everyone to munch on while we watched a
movie in the boys' room. Julian needed to work at the orphanage the
following day, leaving us an entire day with Juan David to ourselves.

I can't say that I even watched the movie. I barely took my
eyes off of that boy. I could hardly believe he was with us. Watching
him interact with his brother was priceless. Julian loved having him
near as well.

Weariness finally took over, so I headed upstairs as soon as
the movie ended. I hugged Julian goodnight and told him I loved
him like I made a habit of doing every night. Juan David caught my
eye, walked over to me, and let me hug him goodnight too.

"Good night. I love you." The words came back so naturally.

"I love you, too." It had been such a long time since I'd heard
him say those words.

I knew I still loved him, I'd just forgotten how much . . . until
then.

Julian left very early the next morning, so I woke up to see him
off. I made a cup of coffee and sat down at the table to enjoy the

solitude. I'm so used to long, quiet mornings on Saturdays because Mike and David can usually sleep the entire morning away.

Juan David emerged from the room pretty early, though, not sure what type of greeting to expect from me or how he should greet me, either. He was a little restless since his brother was gone, and he couldn't go back to sleep.

I gave him a hug, asked him how he slept, and told him about our plans for the day.

"Mike and David will likely sleep for a long while still, so you can watch TV in the bedroom until they wake up." I didn't quite know how to react to another early riser. He went back in the bedroom to watch some Spanish cartoon movies we brought from home.

After a little while, I realized I'd waited too long for this very morning, one that wouldn't come by me again anytime soon. I walked into the bedroom and found him all curled up in the blanket watching Superman. I sat down beside him and watched with him for a while.

Honestly, I didn't know what to do or say to this child. It had been so long, and so much happened over the last two-and-a-half years since the last time we were allowed to talk over the phone.

I finally loosened up a bit. I wrapped my arm around him, and I told him again I loved him.

"I love you, too. *Mucho* (a lot)." He gently leaned his head onto my shoulder.

"I've missed you," I told him in all honesty.

"I've missed you, too. *Hartísimo.* (Incredibly)." He tenderly responded.

We sat there together, his head on my shoulder, my head tilted to rest on top of his curly hair. It felt like a dream. One of those special moments in time I once accepted would never happen.

We talked on and off through the cartoons, and then I went upstairs to get Mike and David up for the day. I will forever cherish that quiet morning between us as a gift. Not only did our paths cross again, reuniting us, but I knew God gave him back to me—at least for this weekend.

The awkwardness vanished, and we actually picked up right up where we left things off two-and-a-half years ago. I wanted to know what he knew of our intentions at the moment, and I found his social worker already told him about our lawyer trying to reopen the case.

"You know now that we love you and never stopped loving you. But I don't want you to go back after this weekend thinking we're going to adopt you." I looked him tenderly in the eye and explained why it didn't even look possible. "We really want to play a role in your life again, even if it only means being able to call you like before."

His psychologist specifically asked me to prepare him for a no, so I did.

Once Mike and David woke up, Mike and I made breakfast while David and Juan David watched some more cartoons together. It melted my heart to see those two together. All that fear I felt during our first taxi ride disappeared. Juan David treated David so sweetly, and David worked hard at using every bit of Spanish he remembered. I sensed a great day awaiting us.

We found a few low-budget activities to do during the day like heading back to the infamous go-karts, a dollar movie theater, and lunch at our favorite restaurant. We enjoyed every minute of the day, and who really knew if we'd ever share time together like this again.

David and Juan David formed an instant bond with the go-karts. David didn't hide a bit of his excitement when he won his race against Juan David.

Lunch gave us time to enjoy meaningful conversation, helping us get reacquainted after all this time. Surprisingly, it didn't take long. Both Juan David and I had very fond and vivid recollections of nearly all of our telephone conversations from almost three years ago. It surprised me how much he remembered.

Juan David said he liked all kinds of foods, especially desserts. We picked a big banana split off the menu and shared it. Such a sweet moment.

After we returned home, David took out his new red soccer ball to play with Juan David in the courtyard at the apartments. I sat on a little bench to watch. Another moment to cherish, one I never imagined happening. Both of those boys are so passionate about soccer, and Juan David's last "family" even gave him the opportunity to train for a possible future in the sport. He wanted to play professional soccer more than anything. I finally saw his talent for the game up close.

I thought back to the first time I ever mentioned the idea to David of adopting Juan David. Juan David's passion for soccer won David's enthusiasm to pursue his adoption the first time. Whenever I talked to Juan David on the phone, he always asked about David's recent soccer games. These two boys literally waited four years for the opportunity to play soccer together, and now they finally had their chance.

The following day we visited the Baptist church where we met Mercedes our very first weekend in Colombia. We fully intended to visit her earlier, but time completely escaped us. We knew Julian needed to reconnect with her, so we chose to visit her church on our final Sunday.

We still didn't find a new place for Julian to live after the summer, and we knew he only had six weeks left in his current housing situation. For some reason, God wouldn't take Mercedes off my heart, so I knew I needed to let her know of his need. Maybe she knew of some options, possibly someone in the church who could take him in or rent him a room. I sent her an e-mail about it and also planned to mention it to her before we left.

Mercedes' heart overflowed with joy when we arrived at church with both Julian and Juan David. She fondly remembered

Juan David and recalled his genuine interest in learning about Jesus as a child. That touched my own heart. God strategically led us to this particular boy.

While we sat in church, I gave Juan David a Spanish New Testament to look at. He hadn't attended a Protestant church since Mercedes took him with her early in his childhood. He held little memory of that period in his life, so this church seemed very foreign to him. He immediately opened the little Bible to Revelation and stayed glued to it for the rest of the service. I let him keep the Bible, knowing he likely had never owned one before.

Zayde invited us to join her family and a few other people for a picnic in the early afternoon, so we needed to leave pretty quickly after church. Mercedes took a few more moments after the service to express her love to Juan David again. As I hugged her one last time and began to say good-bye a few minutes later, she seemed reluctant to let go.

"When are you leaving Colombia? When do you need to take Juan David back? I want to invite you all to have lunch with me at my house tomorrow."

We thanked God for giving us yet another chance to connect with her before taking Juan David back to the orphanage and then leaving Colombia ourselves. If I could do it over again, I'd spend every weekend with her. Such a genuine, godly woman who loved the same children I did.

We met up with Zayde and the others around one o'clock to head to a quieter area of the city for our picnic. We set up camp, ate, and then all of the guys and a few girls played soccer together for the remainder of the afternoon. Even Julian, not athletically inclined, joined in the game and really enjoyed himself. I loved watching him interact with his brother.

Months passed since Julian had seen Juan David. This may have even been their first opportunity to spend time together somewhere in the presence of a family outside of the orphanage. They both were a gift to us, and God used us to give them a priceless gift of time with each other.

While the "kids" played, Mike and I slipped away with Zayde to a little coffee shop across the street. What a beautiful day, in so many ways.

When we finally came home that evening, we picked up a few specific things Julian wanted to buy to make us a special dinner. He usually stayed out of the kitchen as much as possible for the entire thirty days, so this gesture really touched us.

He made us baked plantains with cheese and a sweet, jelly-like spread inside. He also cooked beans, but the final product really disappointed him. The beans tasted too salty and did not cook long enough, and he wished he fried the plantains rather than baking them.

"Julian, it all still tastes really good! We are so proud of you!" We tried our best to encourage him to step out and try new things.

"No. I am never going to make any of this again." We learned quickly that this boy did not accept failure well. Rather than learning from mistakes, he ran away from them.

The next morning, we made a huge batch of French toast (David's favorite) for the boys to try for breakfast. Juan David devoured every bite of it. We lounged around the apartment, soaking up our final morning with Juan David. We looked forward to our lunch invitation at Mercedes' house, but it saddened all of us to know we only had a few hours left with Juan David. We'd waited too long for this weekend to become a reality. Every moment needed to count.

We reminisced with Juan David over one of the weekends we spent with him and his sister four years before in Austin, Texas. We talked about the restaurant where we'd eaten and the splash park the kids played in with David. He even remembered every detail of our conversation the day we stood on a bridge over a small pond looking at turtles.

Right before we left home to come to Colombia this time, I found yet another set of the pictures we'd taken that day in a small photo album. We pulled them out to show them to Juan David that last morning together.

His eyes lit up when he saw the pictures. He recalled every moment of that summer in Texas. The surprise and gratitude written all over his face when I said he could keep them were priceless. If I had the chance to stay in another country for a summer at the age of ten, I sure would have wanted at least a few pictures to remember the experience. These kids didn't own a single picture of their childhood. Period.

After our lazy morning together, we left to go to Mercedes' house. Juan David admitted he had very little memory of her, though he recognized her at church. He didn't remember her family, her home, or anything about her. As the taxi pulled up to her house, the memories started coming back.

She let us in the front door of her house and immediately hugged all over those two boys. "Do you remember all the times you spent here as children?"

Juan David looked around and remembered the chair in the living room where he always fell asleep. Memories suddenly flooded his mind as we toured the rest of the house. "I remember playing with cars on the floor of this room. I also remember that you took us to church with you every week."

Julian didn't stop smiling because he felt so at home. I couldn't get over how God continued to reveal their story to us, filling in gap after gap. Mercedes told me about Julian's learning difficulties as a child and all the time she spent teaching him how to read and write. Her memories matched everything he'd already told me about her. How amazing to actually be in the same location where all those stories took place, in the very same home where they played as children.

Mercedes now knew about Julian's upcoming need for housing. While we toured the house, she showed him an upstairs room where he could stay if he'd like.

"You always have a home here with me." She smiled directly at Julian. I knew in that moment we found where he belonged, surrounded by people who knew him, loved him, and understood him.

She knew where he came from, something more than we could ever offer him. A miracle.

Gathered around her table, we enjoyed a traditional Colombian lunch together, one specific to Bogotá. A three potato soup, garnished with corn on the cob, bananas, and avocado. We tried it several times before, but her recipe tasted the best so far. Even David enjoyed it, though he only really drank the broth. For dessert she served us little figs she picked from her tree and boiled in sugar water. They were delicious!

I cherished the conversation with her and her family and considered it an honor to share this lunch with them. We also thoroughly enjoyed watching so many memories come alive for those boys. Juan David had forgotten all of the biblical foundations she'd given him as a child, but it didn't take her long to fill him in on the whole plan of salvation while we sat at her table together.

Sadly, we only stayed for a few hours in order to get Juan David back to the orphanage on time that afternoon. We requested to keep him until Monday evening because we needed all of Tuesday to resituate Julian in his home before we flew back to the United States early Wednesday morning.

"What? You're not leaving until Wednesday? Why can't I stay with you one more night?" When Juan David heard we weren't leaving on Tuesday, he begged for more time with us.

Julian made a few phone calls to the orphanage to ask permission for us to keep him one more night. Juan David jumped up and down with excitement when they said it would be okay. I don't think he stopped hugging me all evening, expressing his gratitude to be with us.

In one short weekend, I'd already grown accustomed to his arms being wrapped around my neck or shoulders every little chance he got.

"Mom, Mom, Mom, Mom, Mom." He started the weekend calling me Rachelle, but when he heard his brother call me Mom, he followed suit and called me Mom the rest of the weekend.

I wished I could let him call me his mom, but I needed to bring him back to earth. He could count on me to love him forever, but it didn't mean we could adopt him. It didn't mean I could be the mom I always wanted to be to him.

So, with one last evening together, we rearranged our plans of how to get Julian's things transported back to his house the following morning. We wanted to make every last hour count, despite our bare kitchen and dwindling bank account. We found an inexpensive pizza place around the corner, so we ordered two large pizzas to take back home with us.

After devouring every last bite of that scrumptious pizza, we agreed it was the best pizza we found there (besides the homemade pizza a fellow missionary made us once). While we ate, we played a little Spanish conversational game I brought with me, taking turns reading and answering questions about ourselves on a little card.

Those little questions helped us learn a lot about each other that evening. Juan David's answers showed that he lived and breathed to get the pretty girls' attention everywhere he went—typical for a 14-year-old boy. We learned David knew how to read in Spanish and actually pronounce the words very well. I helped him understand the questions, but I was so impressed with his ability to read in another language. No one ever taught him, so I still to this day wonder how he knew.

We also learned Julian really did like to talk and open up, contrary to his closed-off attitude the entire month we were together. We became so used to him not even wanting to sit at the table together because he always wanted to be alone, and yet he answered every question with more detail than we ever wanted to know. We didn't realize his need to be prompted with random questions or to be put on the spot. What a great family-oriented experience for us to share together our last night.

Tuesday morning turned out quite complicated, leading to an extremely busy day. We all woke up early to empty out the fridge and cabinets and get Julian and Juan David all packed up. I don't think Julian realized the finality of this day because we struggled to get him to pack everything.

Getting to his house proved challenging, too. We couldn't find a taxi big enough to carry all five of us in addition to all the luggage. Getting on a bus with all that stuff just wasn't safe. So, we all grabbed a backpack and carried at least one bag of food in the other hand. We gave Julian all the food that remained in the kitchen.

Mike took charge of the large suitcase on wheels, and Juan David carried the soccer ball David gave him. After a forty minute walk through Bogotá, we made it to Julian's house. What an adventure! Mike and David led the way, quickly, while I took up the rear again with the other two boys.

We dropped off all the suitcases and backpacks, let Juan David meet the lady Julian lived with, and gave him a quick little tour of the house. How priceless for Juan David to see Julian's room with all the pictures of his siblings on the wall above his bed.

The very pictures I took down from my own wall at home to give to Julian, the same pictures Juan David now owned.

Julian didn't forget about his siblings after they all went separate ways. Not for a second.

10

SAYING GOOD-BYE WITH HOPE

"I will not leave you as orphans; I will come to you."
John 14:18

How Do I Let Go Again?

I let you go once,
Then I let you go again.
Another family would soon adopt you
Though we all kept wondering when.

I only asked for one thing
Before they took you away.
I asked God to somehow let me
Hear from you again someday.

He urged you to write a letter
That your brother later sent to me.
Then I gratefully accepted
You had a new family.

Yet when things didn't work out for you
I begged God to tell me why.
I asked him to reunite us
Long after we'd said good-bye.

Now here we are, face to face,
Having to bid good-bye once more.
This time I won't let you go,
Hoping a final reunion is still in store.

Our time soon ran out. We needed to get Juan David back to the orphanage.

We all tried to keep our spirits up during our final taxi ride together, but the mood quickly changed, and the sad reality set in. Our time was up, and no one really knew when or if we'd ever see each other again.

We were supposed to have another meeting with our lawyer and the two men from the Family Welfare Office, this time with Juan David's social worker present, but that meeting never took place. We hoped to at least hear something back from our lawyer regarding the status of our case, but we heard nothing. We had no idea if reopening our case was even a possible reality, and I couldn't even promise Juan David we would stay in touch because I didn't have any answers yet.

I kept my arm around that little guy the whole ride back to the orphanage. He reached up his hand and grabbed one of my fingers resting upon his shoulder, holding onto it the whole way. This weekend had been a gift we would all cherish in our hearts.

My own heart beat nervously as we finally approached that familiar street, and I dreaded stepping out of the taxi. I didn't know how to say good-bye.

I'm sure Julian experienced a lot of mixed feelings as well. He had permission to call his brother twice a week on the same nights I used to call him, but he wasn't able to visit or see him either. This was good-bye for him too.

Every pair of eyes in the room followed us as soon as we walked into Juan David's house. He carried his backpack and soccer ball upstairs, while I took in the scene around me. All of those children gathered in the room where they would spend the rest of the day together.

Girls and boys alike, all different ages, all with a story as to why they were there instead of at home with their family. Some of them truly orphaned, some abandoned like Juan David and Julian, some abused terribly, and some had run away from an unspeakable home environment. Several of them underwent therapy with their families in order to reunite one day. Others dealt with losses greater than we could ever imagine. Many wondered if their turn would ever come to join a family through adoption.

My heart broke.

Juan David came back downstairs, and we all gave him one last hug.

"We love you." As soon as he pulled away from my embrace, he walked over to the other children gathered in the room, never once turning back to look as we walked out of his home. I sensed he'd done this many times before, especially with the last family that didn't end up working out. He'd learned to say good-bye and not look back, to just keep moving forward.

Survival.

These kids demonstrated great coping skills. Their ability to survive would serve them well in the future, while their inability to embrace emotion would prove detrimental in other areas of their lives. We sadly saw all of that in Julian's life over the last five months since he'd exited "the system." Scarred for life.

The more they are abandoned, let down, or disappointed, the more they withdraw into themselves, believing they can't trust anyone. They subconsciously build walls around their hearts as a way to protect themselves from ever having to feel the hurt cut more deeply than it had before. We witnessed this reality in Julian, and we hoped Juan David now knew we never chose to abandon him.

We prayed our time together would light up his dark world and that knowing how much we still loved him would comfort his lonely heart. Knowing how dearly he still loved us comforted our own hearts. We needed him in our lives as much as he needed us to stay in his life. We walked away from that orphanage hopeful to hear positive news soon.

I held on tightly to David as we rode the bus back to the apartment. This, too, would be our final bus ride for the summer. Fortunately, I had a ton on my mind about all we still had left to do over the next few hours. My mom-mode kicked into gear, making a mental checklist of how to get it all done the most efficiently. Had I not been so preoccupied, I don't know how I would have emotionally survived the ride home. My heart ached for the boy we had to leave behind.

When we got back to the apartment, we packed all of our stuff and began our cleaning spree. In order to save money, we agreed to clean the apartment on our own before we left. We cleaned out the entire kitchen, scrubbed the bathrooms, emptied all the trash, washed the bedding, returned the borrowed mattress and bedding, and swept the floors. All our luggage sat ready by the door so we could leave before six o'clock the next morning.

Julian stayed with us again that final night, so he kept one last backpack full of necessities with him, plus his mini-laptop. He cleaned his own bathroom and swept most of the apartment. While Julian and I finished up most of the cleaning and shared one of those good, heart-to-heart talks about the future, David and Mike walked to the little bakery around the corner to purchase our breakfast for the next morning. Fortunately, our Colombian friends who used to serve at our church back home in Texas invited us over for dinner at their apartment later in the evening, so we didn't need to worry about where or what to eat that night.

How nice to reconnect with "family" from our home church. We also appreciated their wisdom and specific Colombian advice for Julian's situation and future. We left them a copy of our book as a gift for the role they played in our journey. Assuring them we'd come back, either for another visit or to possibly complete an adoption, we bid our good-byes. The next morning would come all too quickly.

Surprisingly, I actually slept, despite all the anxiety building up inside me. I hated good-byes. We woke up super early to wash the sheets and hang them to dry. While we ate our last breakfast, the P.E. Coach from the school stopped by. He gave us some letters to mail for him in the States, and he prayed with us before we left. He also brought a little cash gift for David, thanking him for his assistance in the P.E. classes in summer school. They formed a very sweet bond over our time in Colombia.

When our ride to the airport showed up promptly at 5:45 a.m. and loaded our luggage into the little van, reality hit me. Saying good-bye to Julian this time meant cutting the strings. We knew we had to comply with his social worker's recent request to pull back the financial support. He needed to look for work, and as long as any money still came from us, he didn't push himself as much as he could.

We hugged him good-bye and told him we loved him, but we didn't even leave him money to take a taxi back home. All the money he had for the next month was what little the orphanage paid him the week before. I knew he had some floundering days ahead, and it broke my heart.

Our own bank account dwindled pretty low, though, so I thanked God for not really giving me a choice in the matter. With Mike taking an unpaid leave of absence to stay two extra weeks in Colombia, we no longer had anything extra to give him anyway. What remained in our savings wouldn't even begin to cover the possible adoption expenses looming overhead.

Difficulty definitely awaited him, but we knew we left him with many strong contacts and connections to turn to whenever he found himself in need. We'd completely taken care of him for the last four months since he took his first steps away from the orphanage on his own. Now began the tough love, pulling ourselves away and forcing him to use the resources God gave him to make his own choices from here.

Even if the Adoption Committee did reopen our case and things moved quickly enough to adopt him too, he needed these next few months to learn to survive without us, to gain more of a sense of responsibility for himself. (Thankfully, Juan David confirmed his true age to us, showing that we had more than a year to complete his adoption before time ran out. He was still only fourteen years old.)

We said good-bye to both of those boys in the last twenty-four hours, but we did so with hope. Maybe one, or even both of them, would legally become our son. God would not leave them as orphans. If he didn't send us back to them, he himself would go to them. No matter what, our intertwined stories would continue to reveal God's ultimate glory.

11

ONE STEP AT A TIME

"When my spirit grows faint within me,
it is you who know my way."
Psalm 142:3a

Here We Go AGAIN

Every night I go to sleep
Not knowing what tomorrow might bring
Not knowing where God will take me
Or what song he'll give me to sing.

I don't want to be the driver
In this adventure with my Lord.
I've thrown out all my plans,
Yet he never leaves me bored!

I'm walking down a yellow brick road
Yet only one brick lies ahead
Until I step upon it,
The next direction remains unsaid.

I don't know what the plan is
Or what the future will hold
Yet he lights my every step
And guides me to treasures untold.

Sometimes it's a little scary
Not knowing where the next step will be,
But I've learned to trust my Driver
Because I trust his plans for me.

July 4, 2012. After a four-hour delay in the El Dorado airport in Bogotá, we finally boarded our first plane home. We actually really enjoyed ourselves for those four hours, spending the rest of our Colombian cash at all the little duty-free shops. The delay left David pretty disappointed, though, because now we wouldn't make it home in time to watch the fireworks that night. July Fourth is one of his favorite holidays.

We arrived in Atlanta, passed quickly through customs and immigration, and soon found ourselves on our next flight home to Dallas.

"I can see the fireworks!" David's eyes lit up with excitement toward the end of our flight. I looked out the window to see little fireworks displays lighting the sky with color all over the place. What a cool experience to look down at the fireworks rather than up. They seemed tiny in comparison to how they look when you're on the ground.

David did get to see the fireworks, after all. God didn't let him down.

The first few days back in Texas felt odd. I always struggle adjusting back to life at home after spending time in another country. I expected to be extremely emotional, to miss everything and everyone in Colombia, and to battle reverse culture shock upon reentering US culture. Yet surprisingly, I felt none of that. It felt so good to be home.

I didn't realize how much I missed home this time around. I took a bath and didn't want to get back out. I wanted to make several cups of coffee with my individual cup brewer every morning. I wanted to eat at my favorite fast-food chicken place as soon as possible. I went to my local discount grocery store, almost ecstatic over how much I bought for so little cost! It brought such satisfaction to fill up my refrigerator and freezer with only a small amount of money. I craved normalcy and routine.

My gratitude for a monolingual home even surprised me. As much as I've always wanted a bilingual home, I felt relieved at no longer having to translate for everyone or be interrupted by a conversation going on in one language by someone trying to start a conversation with me in another language.

I kept waiting for a longing for Colombia to return, but it didn't.

I honestly never experienced such a pleasant return to my own culture before. I expected to feel homesick for Colombia, her ways, and her people, but I wasn't, and I didn't know why. Little by little, I descended into a new valley, filled with emotions (or a lack of emotions) I never expected.

David and I had a few days to hang out and chill together before he left for church camp. Summer is our sacred time to find all kinds of adventures and build unique memories, just the two of us. He felt positive about pursuing this adoption, but we both obviously carried mixed emotions.

Our lawyer finally contacted us again, two days after we returned home. He said the men already presented our case to the

Head of Adoptions, so we might receive an answer within another week or so. We learned a week could actually mean several, though. But we also learned what a difference it made to have our own attorney.

We prepared ourselves to hear it couldn't legally be done, possibly our way of guarding our hearts. An e-mail from our lawyer surprised us in more ways than one when it arrived only three days later, saying the Adoption Committee did reopen our case!

To start, they requested only two things: a new psychological evaluation including David, and a new home study to approve us for both boys, in case we didn't run out of time for Julian. We would need to send the documents via a Colombian-approved adoption agency. If they deemed us approvable in those reports, then we could finish out the process.

This actually added more time to the process, but it made sense. We didn't need to collect every single document again and spend all that money only to find out they still didn't like what they saw in those two reports. The psychological evaluations and the home study would cost us enough!

By this point, *we knew that we knew that we knew.* God did this. God performed an absolute miracle by reopening our case for this boy. He led us directly to our attorney. He allowed us to meet the very men who denied us, after all this time. He preserved our relationship with Juan David and directly involved us in Julian's life precisely when his brother's second chance for a family fell through.

A closed door didn't intimidate God. He opened it right before our very eyes. How could we live with ourselves by refusing to walk through it?

Yet despite it all, we still struggled immensely with the thought of going through the adoption process again. I mean, who does this? Who gets pushed face down to the ground, yet goes back for more? Faith had to lead the way or my fears would completely swallow me. The anxiety would have eaten me alive. If God didn't make it so obvious, I don't think I could have done it.

As Beth Moore stated in her study, *Children of the Day,*[3] (p. 42) "The prospect of putting ourselves at risk again can be terrifying. . . When God opens the door again, let's stand back up, brush ourselves off, and step through it. In that wild place of getting back up, a wonder can occur: our God can embolden us."

I didn't realize how much I guarded my heart, protecting myself from inevitable hurt, the way those kids in the orphanage learned to cope. Last time around, I felt like doing cartwheels or jumping up and down screaming the day I found out we could pursue the adoption. Each step of the process brought incredible joy. This time, fear gripped me.

I expected that joy again, mixed with gratitude.

I only found fear. I was terrified.

Stepping through that open door led straight into one of the loneliest valleys we'd ever walked, so contrary to the first process being a mountaintop experience. With God as our guide, our lamp, and our light, we obediently followed into the valley, one step at a time. I clung to him with everything in me.

I went through a whirlwind of emotions over those next few days, scrambling to get things moving as quickly as possible. We followed the yellow brick road in front of us. Enough light showed us the next step to take, but we had no idea where the path headed or when it might reach a destination. We followed, one day at a time.

Not so easy with so many onlookers, whispering or even shouting hurtful comments and insults along the way. We heard and felt them all, even those spoken behind our backs or mumbled under someone's breath.

"You're crazy! Why would you even think of going through all that again?"

"You're wasting all of your money and your time!"

"It's not worth the risk."

Most said things out of pure ignorance. So many voices fought for our attention. But we knew, and we trained our ears to listen to the only voice that mattered.

Mike took over making phone calls, while I took charge in the electronic department, contacting people via e-mail. Within a few days, we found out our original home study agency closed a few years ago, meaning we had no choice but to complete an entirely new home study. An update for $800 quickly turned into a minimum of $3,000 for a new home study and post-placement fees.

We set up a new psychological evaluation with a recommended psychologist. With David's evaluation added this time, it would cost over a thousand dollars. We'd already dipped into our savings to enjoy our four days with Juan David, and now our funds ran short for the following month due to Mike's unpaid leave of absence.

We live frugally, with more than enough in a separate savings account most of the time. Unexpected car problems, house repairs, school expenses, etc. don't stress us because we usually have the funds to cover them. Paying up front for these two reports left our savings account with only fifty-three dollars. A friend gave us some cash on two occasions to help out, bringing it up to $153.

The security of knowing we had spare funds suddenly vanished. I, of course, feared the worst. The cars. The house. Medical emergencies. I'm sure glad I didn't know how long those numbers would actually remain stuck at $153. By stripping us of our financial security, God taught us to depend completely on him.

So, we scheduled our psychological evaluations and home study. Now we needed a Colombian-approved international adoption agency. Meaning thousands of dollars more.

On an empty bank account.

The two men in Colombia recommended we use the same agency as before. They said finding a different agency might look bad, like we had something to hide.

We honestly couldn't afford to start over with a new agency even if we'd wanted. Our original agency's fees were the most reasonable. Yet I can't say we parted with our agency on the best of terms. We didn't blame them for our denial, but we felt they didn't advocate well for us, nor did they comply with our requests throughout our appeal and after. I even filed a complaint against them for not giving me a translation I requested (which we received shortly after). If we followed the suggestion to use the same agency, we wondered if the agency would even agree to take us back.

Mike called the director of the agency and explained the newest changes in our case. She hesitated at first, but she did agree to work with us again. In fact, she didn't charge us a penny (other than for translation) until we knew if Colombia even approved our first two reports. On top of that, she found us a grant for $3,000 to cover the majority of the program fees.

We knew God chose this road for us, but we felt like fools at the same time. Did we dare face this monster again? Every possible negative effect this might have on David, on our marriage, and on our finances threatened to steal any peace of mind I had.

I kept my eye glued to the numbers on our bank account, realizing that humanly speaking, this was a ridiculous move. God and God alone could fund this crazy operation a second time, or it would wipe us out completely.

Again, who does this?

I begged God every day to provide for our needs so we would have enough. I soon received a check in the mail from a friend wanting to contribute a little late to our trip. Other friends took it upon themselves to cover our meal costs whenever we went out to eat for church functions. Another friend helped out with cash, the money that kept our savings account afloat through the next year. A complete stranger in line behind me at the grocery store paid for my entire cart of groceries. A friend passed on enough clothing to make our closets and shelves completely overflow. Someone else even wrote us a check for several hundred dollars to cover our translation fees throughout the rest of the process.

We couldn't argue our case. God provided.

Meanwhile, Julian completely ran out of both money and food. I carried his burdens on my shoulders until my new friend and mentor, Mercedes, assured me God had him covered. She invited him to eat lunch with her several times, and I know several others invited him to eat on other occasions. He had to scramble for crumbs at times, but at least we knew the people around him would not let him starve.

Now we had an international agency, appointments with a psychologist, and an agreement signed with a local home study agency. The psychologist worked with us to schedule an appointment as quickly as possible. We had a tight schedule ahead of us in order to attempt to get Julian, too, which I still did not believe possible.

A race against the clock. Julian's window of opportunity would expire at the end of November. That left us only four months to get these reports done, apostilled, translated, and reviewed by Colombia (adding apostille fees, airmail fees, and translation fees), plus be fingerprinted and approved for Part A with immigration (another $900) in order to file his paperwork for Part B by the deadline. Getting approval for Part A alone could take up to ninety days.

We also needed to secure official documents from Julian to prove he and Juan David were siblings. Even if we got all of that done in such a short window of time, we still had more paperwork to gather in order to complete our file and receive an official approval from Colombia after that. Some days we felt like complete idiots for even attempting it, yet somehow we knew we had to.

Colombia's Adoption Committee denied our first adoption attempt due to a personality assessment which made Mike look completely detached from and afraid of the world. They also didn't like a comment about David's nervousness to share a room. We later found out we took a personality assessment much different from the norm, so they read it much differently than a psychologist familiar with the test would read it. This time we made sure to take the right test so we knew they would read it correctly.

I was a nervous wreck while taking the test, answering five hundred plus questions about myself. Meanwhile Mike took the test across the wall from me, and David took a child's version of the test in yet another room. Our interviews seemed to go well, but David's interview made me nervous because Colombia wanted to make sure he no longer harbored nervous feelings regarding the adoption.

What ten-year-old child who has grown up without siblings would not feel nervous? That healthy nervousness led us into some very serious discussions to prepare his little heart for the many possible changes. We hoped the psychologist would pick up on that and reflect it positively in his report.

Ten days later, a very positive psychological evaluation arrived at our doorstep. Our personality assessments did not even hint at the negatives the evaluators read in the last ones we'd taken. Plus, the psychologist pointed out that David's original nervousness only came from his high intelligence and ability to consider all the pros and cons of a given situation. What sweet relief!

Now we focused on the home study. We started filling out the paperwork as soon as it came in the mail. Thankfully, we found we already had almost all of the documents needed for it. We had everything ready to send within a few days, besides our medical forms and employment letters. The lady said to send those later, so we mailed the packet right away in order to get our home study scheduled as quickly as possible.

While waiting to hear from a social worker to set up our home study interviews, we filled out our employment letters and medical forms. We had to get tested for HIV and tuberculosis, as well as for other blood-related illnesses. I'd recently had a physical, so my doctor filled out my form right away. Mike's doctor wouldn't fill it out without Mike getting all of his blood work done for a full physical. Our insurance didn't cover most blood tests, so another significant bill came in the mail shortly after. Hundreds of dollars. Ouch.

In all of this stress, I kept losing sight of the fact that God controlled this boat. We didn't race against anyone or anything. His future for those boys would happen no matter what. The possibilities for both of their adoptions were miracles in and of themselves. Two doors that could never open, or so they said.

Only God brought us to this point, period. I wish I kept that at the front of my mind rather than getting so overwhelmed by all the details and the voices shouting out at me that this couldn't be done. I only needed to listen to one voice, the voice of Truth.

The only way to make it through this process emotionally was by seeking that voice of Truth first thing every morning. I had to seek him rather than some preconceived outcome. He was the One who "armed me with strength for the battle" (Ps. 18:39a).

When I sought him first and foremost, his outcome always prevailed, without me getting in the way. It always turned out better than the one I had preconceived, anyway. If I wanted to make it through this lonely valley, I had to let go of the reins, precisely what I learned the last time we walked through the valley. How quickly we forget.

12

HIS TIMING AND PROVISION

"The one who calls you is faithful, and he will do it."
1 Thessalonians 5:24

Not My Load to Carry

Running out of money
Running low on fuel
Running out of time
Running out of tools

My energy's depleted
My emotions all maxed out
My insecurities overwhelm me
I didn't want to take this route!

Didn't we sacrifice enough
The first time we walked this road?
"Child, when did I ever leave you
Or ask you to carry this God-sized load?"

Gentle whispers reminded me
He continued to be our guide.
He carried this load on his shoulders
And faithfully walked by our side.

Three long weeks passed before our social worker even called
to set up our home study interviews. Thankfully, she came only a
few days after calling. I really hoped to have this part behind us
before school started in mid-August, but no such luck. She came
on a Sunday afternoon, and I started a week of staff development
meetings the next day.

She interviewed Mike and me together, which seemed to go
pretty well. Our situation was complicated, so it took a bit of effort
to explain it all. She toured the house to confirm the safety of our
environment, and then she said she'd come back on Wednesday
afternoon to complete the individual interviews.

David suddenly felt a moment of panic in those few days of
waiting for his own individual interview. He knew how the last social
worker's comment about his nervousness impacted Colombia's
decision to deny us. We didn't realize what a weight he carried on
himself this time, scared that one wrong word might bring it all down.
Our family faced quite a bit of spiritual warfare over that three-day
wait. We breathed a huge sigh of relief as soon as she left our home
on Wednesday evening.

We assumed she understood our specific time crunch, yet
another three weeks passed before she sent us her written report.
After we carefully reviewed it in search of any errors, we sent a

corrected copy back for her to sign within a few hours. She signed it and then sent it to the home study agency for final editing and review before our own international agency could approve it.

Meanwhile, we sent a scanned copy of our psychological report to our international agency, and our caseworker found two specific comments they wanted changed or reworded. Our psychologist willingly made the corrections and sent a new report rather quickly. He completely understood our timing issues with Julian, as he himself had come to the United States from Canada in a similar situation.

Time ticked on while we waited for our home study agency to finish editing our final home study. They claimed our report was a top priority, but still days and weeks passed by. When we finally got it, we understood why it had taken so long.

For immigration purposes and because of strict laws under the Hague Convention, we couldn't mention having had any recent contact with Juan David. Our social worker wrote our story exactly as it happened, so they needed to change huge parts of her first report. Basically, they took Juan David's name completely out of it.

The revised report now described our weekend with Juan David and Julian simply as a weekend visit to the orphanage. Considering we've never spent an entire weekend there, we hoped it didn't send a red flag once it got to Colombia. Our international agency approved and apostilled it right away without giving us a chance to object. Besides, we didn't have time to argue about it. We had to send it to Immigration as soon as possible.

Every day counted. Immigration could take up to ninety days to approve us, yet less than sixty remained between now and November 30.

Still possible? Yes.

Probable? No.

We hoped to have already sent both reports to Colombia by now to know if we could even continue the process. I hated the thought of dropping another nine hundred dollars in fees to Immigration without an answer from Colombia first, but we didn't have any other choice. We couldn't wait.

If we waited, we wasted all of our time even putting Julian in the paperwork. We bit the bullet, wrote the check, and prayed to make it through the month financially. By the time we sent it, only fifty days remained before Nov. 30.

As we should have assumed would happen, we had other unexpected glitches arise with our paperwork, keeping those two reports from getting to Colombia until early November. *Nothing went as planned.* We never hit any roadblocks threatening to halt the whole operation, but each little bump in the road continually delayed the process.

November. The month holding so many answers.

I can't even begin to describe the daily battle I fought between faith and anxiety. I taught a Bible study on Esther[4] on Wednesday evenings, and I'm convinced the author of the study wrote the specific message each week just for me, for *such a time as this.* I connected deeply with the character of Esther, as I anxiously awaited life-changing news like she did. By the end of the study, I felt as if I knew her personally.

13

A PSYCHOLOGICAL ROLLERCOASTER

"Wait for the Lord. Be strong and take
heart and wait for the Lord."
Psalm 27:14

Holding My Breath

A surprising change of events
Once more life turns upside down.
Could our reversal of destiny
Finally come around?

Do I dare to actually believe
We might win this race against time?
Dare I even assume
We have strength enough for the climb?

First the expenses overwhelm me,
Incredible anxiety rises within.
What a risk we're taking
With a budget already so thin.

Haven't we given enough to this point,
Sacrificed more than our share?
This burden feels so heavy,
Almost more than I can bear.

No surplus of money exists,
Only provision enough for each day.
Time continually ticks against us,
As fear steals hope away.

I am terrified of the outcome,
Whichever way God may lead.
Terrified we've made a mistake,
Terrified we might succeed.

What a grueling journey before us
I hold my breath as we trudge through.
We face an impossible task,
Something only God can do.

I try lifting my hands in surrender,
I try to give in to defeat,
Yet God keeps pushing forward,
Giving no chance to retreat.

We know he's up to something
Grander than we can even dream.
So we hold our breath through this process,
Remembering God holds up our team.

As we near the end of the timeline,
With only a few days that remain.
God pushes through like a whirlwind,
With power no one can feign.

He connects it all together,
Proving again his ultimate control.
He's turned the tables in our story,
And gave back more than the enemy stole.

I breathe a bit more easily now.
Relief is written all over my face.
Yet God knew all along
He'd already won this race.

November 6, 2012. Juan David's fifteenth birthday. Three years before on this very day, I said good-bye for the last time. I still called a few more times after that, only to hear an excuse as to why he couldn't talk to me. I assumed the excuses were meant to discourage my calls, so I stopped calling.

I was right. He stood by the phone every time and listened to each excuse. He knew all along I didn't abandon him by choice.

Three years later, I now held the phone in my hand and dialed his number again. I had permission to call him twice a month for the last two months. We didn't talk about a possible adoption. We didn't talk about the future. We simply reacquainted ourselves. I felt so grateful for the opportunity to celebrate his special day with him.

Julian once told me their birthdays pass by like any other day while they're in the orphanage. No celebration. No recognition. It's just another day.

Not to me. This birthday wouldn't pass him by unnoticed by the people who loved him the most.

I called him while at the soccer field because David had a game that evening. We both remembered his birthday as the last time we talked before things fell apart. Now we talked soccer again and reminisced over many of our previous conversations from previous years. Both of us treasured this present conversation.

The month started with a blessing, and it continued to hold more and more promise. The director of our international adoption agency told me the day before to call Immigration to see if they might consider expediting our case because of our circumstances with Julian. She called on our behalf first, but the person on the other end of the line coldly told her they had ninety days to approve our case.

"It would be best if you called them directly. Maybe hearing from you personally will make a difference." She was right.

I called the Immigration officer assigned to us and attempted to explain our circumstances to the lady, but I ended up having to forward her the entire page from their own website to show her where the November 30 deadline even came from. We obviously had a unique situation.

"Could you forward me a copy of Julian's birth certificate?" She said she'd need to see proof of his age. I went home on my conference time to find his birth certificate in all of my documents and scan it to her. By the time I sent it, she'd already gone home, so she didn't even receive it until the next day.

"I got your e-mail this morning, but I need you to translate that birth certificate into English." It was already midday. Ugh. I asked if I needed an official translator, but she said if I could do it, that would be fine.

A day later, before I even got it translated, she called me on her own.

"I just wanted you to know that I'm approving your case right now. It looks like you've got quite a time crunch on your hands, so you better get busy!" Her voice hinted at her enthusiasm to help us.

Thankfully we already got our fingerprints done the week before, despite walking in three weeks before our scheduled appointment. What could have taken up to three months barely took three weeks. Now we still had time to file Julian's paperwork for Part B of the Immigration process before the end of the month!

A miracle indeed. Could we safely believe God had this one covered, that Julian would legally become part of our family?

Two weeks later, our attorney e-mailed me very early on Thanksgiving morning. He said the psychologist and social worker over our case in Colombia asked for us to send the rest of our documents so they could make an official decision on our adoption. Based on our psychosocial reports, they did not see any reason to deny us this time!

Our Thanksgiving miracle. I think I glowed all day. We needed this confirmation before filing Julian's paperwork with Immigration, which we did the following day. We hoped it would freeze his status while we wrapped things up for Juan David's adoption.

So far, the door for Julian remained open, despite all the reasons we believed it would shut completely by the end of the month.

The last few documents we needed to collect might take about four to eight more weeks to secure. The simple stuff: birth certificates, marriage license, medical letters, employment letters, FBI fingerprints, and apostilles from three different states.

I ordered my birth certificate online, assured to be the quickest delivery option, the following morning. The state of Indiana did not offer this method, so we ordered Mike's via mail. We requested employment letters from both of our jobs right away. I also dropped off the medical forms at the doctor's office so they could fill them out. Thankfully we had an extra certified copy of our marriage license from last time around. Our international agency had to send us the fingerprint cards for our criminal background check, but I remembered it only took a week to get the results back the last time we'd done them, so they were the least of my concerns.

We couldn't believe our checklist had gotten so small and that this process would be behind us very soon. Maybe before Christmas even!

Not even close. December challenged my faith all over again, despite the miracles we witnessed in November. It went from bad to worse. We ended up with a complicated mess by the end of the month.

To start, we ordered (and paid high postage fees for) the wrong birth certificate for Mike, so we had to order (and pay high postage fees again for) the right one from the right department. My birth certificate never came throughout the entire month. When I called to check on it, they reminded me they had thirty business days to get it to me, adding that Pennsylvania was currently running behind at least another week. They were updating their computer system that month, so they even posted online that there was no way to speed up the printing of vital records.

Mike's employment letter did not get notarized correctly, so they would not apostille it down in Austin until we sent a new one. Our fingerprint cards took a week to get to us. Then it took another four and a half weeks to get the results for our criminal background check with the FBI. Not so fast this time around.

In hindsight, I wish we began this end of the paper chase at the beginning, at least two months before. It would have changed everything.

The paperwork nightmare didn't even compare to the rest of the complications that arose, though. Midway through December, the boys' social worker sent me an e-mail to say I could no longer have any contact with Juan David throughout the process. I also heard they'd had a big meeting about us in Colombia that day to discuss our case, this time with everyone from the orphanage included. My heart sank.

I e-mailed our lawyer to ask him if this news might mean we were still in danger of not being approved after all. Several days later, he responded.

"The main psychologist over your case wants to speak with you directly by phone as soon as possible."

I called almost immediately and talked with him for at least a half hour. Still at school, I was grateful to find a quiet classroom to make the phone call, but I still struggled to hear him when announcements came over the intercom and bells periodically rang.

The psychologist filled me in on the recent meeting by letting me know of their newest requests of us. He asked for more information about how we prepared ourselves to parent a teenager so they could make their decision over whether or not to approve us, but he talked about our future with Juan David like it was already a done deal. However, somehow we'd reached a huge miscommunication point regarding the situation with Julian.

"You can't adopt Julian. He is already an adult and not part of our system anymore. We're not sure why you added him to the paperwork, but you need to take his name completely out of it."

To adopt Julian, his adoption had to take place in the United States, but he could only get here one way, through a younger sibling's adoption. Our attorney helped explain all of it in detail to the two men when we met with them in the summer. Our paperwork also had to include him for Immigration purposes.

No one listened, apparently. This situation was too rare, I guess, for them to even comprehend it. Once they reviewed our paperwork in Colombia with the rest of Juan David and Julian's support team, no one understood why Julian even appeared in our documents.

This psychologist clearly wanted Juan David's adoption to work out, but he acted as if he didn't remember anything we originally explained about the possibility for Julian to immigrate to the States with him.

He was right—we couldn't adopt him *there*. Something like this had been done only a handful of times, so none of them understood that the possibility even existed. I knew we needed our lawyer to explain the situation to him again, but I didn't argue for fear of jeopardizing the positive notes of this phone call.

I also talked to the psychologist more about my on-going relationship with Juan David, and he finally agreed the contact could only benefit everyone. He said he'd try to get me permission to start calling Juan David again, but who knew what a tangled mess it would create to navigate through all of the red tape again. I had to go through three different people on three different levels to regain that permission, leaving Juan David feeling abandoned again for months on end.

That same week, a pink letter arrived in the mail from Immigration. We'd seen this color letter before during our last adoption attempt and knew what it meant. A request for more information.

Unfortunately, they would not freeze Julian's status. The letter gave us until January 14 to send our paperwork for the younger sibling in order to complete the file for an older sibling. Less than a month to finish our process, translate our documents, receive official approval from Colombia, and receive our referral to adopt Juan David, plus gather the documents needed to submit to Immigration.

Absolutely impossible. The director of our international agency said she would help us try to get an extension, but our hearts already accepted Julian likely would not come home to us with Juan David.

To add to all the complication, only a week remained before Christmas. I enjoyed a desperately needed break from work, but everyone else did the same. Everyone in Colombia. Everyone at our agency. Everyone at the Immigration office. Everyone we needed to talk to. No one works the week before Christmas.

Anxiety nearly consumed me my entire break, knowing everything had gotten thrown in the air with nowhere to land. I couldn't talk to anyone! I tried my best to embrace the break as just that—a break. A time to rest and enjoy myself. A few days to reclaim my life. A time to recuperate from all the constant stress. I had no other choice.

"Rest in me, child. Rest in me." I heard his gentle whisper telling me to let him carry my burdens. Somehow I did.

The entire situation regarding my phone calls to Juan David continued to irritate me. I wonder if anyone even thought, or cared, about the timing, cutting this child off from the people he loved right before Christmas.

They wanted proof we completed training on how to deal with children who have attachment disorders, yet they themselves continued to disrupt several of the greatest attachments in his life. Not only with us, but also with his brother and his sister. They say it protects the kids from future heartache. Yet all it does is create more.

I didn't understand the point. It motivated us even more to do all we could to speed up the rest of the process.

I couldn't get in touch with a single person until January 7, the same day I, too, went back to work after the holiday break. I asked our lawyer to re-explain our intentions to adopt Julian with the people over our case. I communicated with our international agency about requesting an extension with Immigration and about details surrounding the needed addendum to our home study to provide the newest information Colombia requested.

We registered for more online training per Colombia's request and asked our home study agency to write an addendum with new information (costing us more than a hundred dollars). Everything came together quickly, except for the extension with Immigration for Julian's case.

"No extensions. You have until January 14 to provide all the documents needed." Her firm voice told me his door was closing quickly.

Our criminal background check finally came back from the FBI, and my birth certificate arrived from Pennsylvania after nearly eight weeks. We sent the background check to our international adoption agency to send for apostille, while we sent the birth certificate to Pennsylvania to be apostilled.

Finally we could send our entire packet of paperwork to Colombia. Meanwhile, I wrote a letter to our immigration officer explaining why we couldn't meet the deadline, accepting a denial for Julian's case.

Conflicted again. Thankful to move forward with Juan David's adoption, thankful at least for some closure regarding Julian. Living up and down was so hard, especially for him. I never did tell him the door officially closed, though.

Much to everyone's surprise, three days later, our immigration officer called me.

"You know what? I made a mistake in the wording of the original paper I sent you. I need to issue you a new one, so that gives you another forty-five days." I detected enthusiasm in her voice again, contrary to the firmness she'd just given me a few days ago.

"Wow. Okay. Thank you." I was stunned.

"I thought you might be happy to hear that." I could almost see the smile on her face as she spoke through the phone.

We now had until March 5 to submit Juan David's paperwork in order to complete Julian's file. Wow. There might be time for him, after all. Could we safely believe Julian would come, too?

The hardest part now lay behind us, or so we thought. No more chasing paperwork. No more making phone calls to this or that agency. No more rearranging schedules in order to intercept a document coming in the mail so we could still send it back out the same day. No more outrageous postage fees. No more online trainings. No more begging for extensions.

Now, we waited.

The Adoption Committee already reviewed our psychosocial reports in November and found us approvable. We assumed the official approval would come fairly quickly. They, themselves, had expressed a desire to get this adoption completed as soon as possible.

A week went by. Then another, and another, and another. The wait was excruciating and psychologically unbearable at times. The loneliest part of the journey so far. Satan used it to tear apart every shred of faith we had. The accusations screamed louder each time.

"How could you be so stupid?"

"No one has ever done this before. They'll never be satisfied with you."

"Now you wiped out your bank account. You stole more time from your only son. You wasted your life on something that can never be. Again."

"You'll never be good enough."

"You went through it all again, and for what? For nothing."

"Juan David will never be your son, and you'll never hear his voice again."

"Julian will never forgive you for dragging him into this, giving him a false hope only to later shatter him."

"You should be ashamed of yourselves." The insults went on and on. Satan tormented me more with each day that passed.

I gave up many lunch times to sit in my classroom alone, as quietly before God as I could, fasting and praying with tears streaming down my cheeks.

"Your will be done. Your will be done. Your will be done." I whispered to God all day long. "We know you led us down this path.

We know that we know that we know. You opened this door. You led us through it. You provided all we needed. You worked miracles on our behalf. You love us, and we know you love these boys."

More than a month passed by, and the weight of anxiety nearly crushed me. I'll never forget the day I walked my class of second-graders to lunch, went back to my classroom, and literally fell straight to my knees in tears as soon as I closed the door behind me.

"God, I need you. *Now.* I can't do this anymore."

Desperately hoping to receive an e-mail that day from our attorney with some kind of answer, I found another one, apparently from God. Only a few minutes after my tearful plea.

"I've seen your sadness. I've heard your cries. A time of gladness is coming." No joke. Another teacher actually sent it, but precisely at the moment I needed it.

Could God have been any more timely? Needless to say, I made it through the day. Later that week, our attorney wrote to congratulate me on the approval of our documents. He hadn't said anything earlier because he still waited for the official paperwork, but now Satan could no longer beat us up.

"In the day when I cried out, you answered me and
made me bold with strength in my soul."
Psalm 138:3

Part Three

...AND TO THE MOUNTAINTOP AGAIN!

14

A LONG RIDE UP

"Be joyful in hope, patient in affliction, faithful in prayer."
Romans 12:12

May I Be . . .

Joyful in hope . . .
May my life be an example
That in the midst of pain is hope,
In the middle of my sorrows
I find a joy to help me cope.

Patient in affliction…
May my life be a testimony
That we have strength to keep pressing on.

Even when we feel like crumbling,
He holds us together till the dawn.

Faithful in prayer...
May my life speak of your presence,
May others want the power they see in me.
When I daily surrender it all in prayer
That's when you set me free.

We finally held that official approval in our hands, a point we'd never reached before. From what they told us, this likely represented the first approval ever issued for a case originally denied, closed, and filed away. We made history!

Neither Mike nor I wanted to get too excited since we had no idea what the road looked like from here to the end. We couldn't celebrate because we still didn't know how much time remained before Juan David, and possibly Julian, came home to us. We finally saw a glimpse of the mountaintop, but little did we know how long it might take to climb back up the mountain. A couple of months, maybe?

Our attorney sent word of our approval at the end of February but didn't get the actual piece of paper until the first week of March. Now we had to wait on the official referral, specifically for Juan David's adoption to arrive before we could complete our paperwork for Part B with Immigration.

Sadly, our forty-five day unexpected extension with Immigration expired, and Julian's door officially closed.

"It really saddens me that things didn't work out for Julian and your family. But I know that everything happens for a reason." This time our immigration officer only typed an e-mail response. By now, she already seemed like a friend instead of an "officer."

Thankfully, Julian had finally found a job and taken more responsibility for his life. He enrolled in a free college to study art and fashion design, the area that captivated his interest and passion. We knew God placed him on a path of his own. He still lived in Mercedes' home, and she insisted he'd be okay right where he was. I still feared the news would crush his heart.

"It's okay, Mom. All I ever really hoped for was for you to successfully adopt my brother." I knew he hid his true disappointment. (Only later did Mercedes confide in me how much the news really devastated him.) I could only hope that our attempt to adopt him at least confirmed how much we loved him.

I hated the fact that I even had to have this conversation with Julian. The reality would soon leave him completely alone in Colombia with both of his siblings gone, but we reminded him he and his brother could stay in contact forever. Plus, we could visit him in the summers like we'd done for the last two years.

Around the same time, we heard about a tour going all across the nation, both to promote international adoption and to point out the flaws in the process that keep so many children separated from the families who love them for far too long. The tour bus would stop in sixty of the nation's largest cities to show a film in a local theater for one night only. They needed a volunteer base in each city to promote the tour and the film by spreading the word throughout the community.

Several people from the adoption ministry in our church joined the team of volunteers in the Dallas area, so Mike and I decided to join too. What a blessing to be amongst other families who also battled through the adoption process and didn't end up with the happy ending you always hear about.

We shared our story of our near five-year journey (still not complete) to bring our son home. Others shared their stories too. A daughter with multiple health problems couldn't come home yet because a new law required more paperwork. A little girl found her family, yet they couldn't even start her adoption process until the country revamps their system. Two little boys in the same orphanage can't get home to their families because their country shut down adoptions with the United States before their adoptions were complete, more than five years ago.

Other parents told about how they used the wait time to prepare their home. They decorated the child's bedroom, filled their closets, and had toys galore waiting for them. Years later, their room still sits empty, while the child still waits.

We'd been there. We knew that heartache.

The journey suddenly didn't seem so lonely. We all had different stories, but we all walked similar trails. Words could not express our gratitude toward the man who started the movement, for taking the risk to give a voice to millions of fatherless children, many who remain fatherless only because of a broken system. We thanked God for connecting us with these new companions as we continued to climb back up the mountain.

Another entire month went by before our referral to adopt Juan David *finally* headed our way. First it had to go through translation before our international adoption agency reviewed it. It finally arrived on our doorstep April 9, meaning we only missed our chance for Julian by a month and four days. Thirty-five days that forever left him legally separated from his brother and a family who loved him. A broken system, indeed.

Receiving that referral finally got things moving again, but so many steps still remained. We officially accepted the referral, submitted the new paperwork to Immigration, waited on more approvals to travel and a date to officially take custody of Juan David. Once we had that date, we needed a new letter written, translated, notarized, and apostilled in order to apply for and secure our travel visas, make our travel arrangements, decide on lodging, and somehow figure out how to pay for our flights, lodging, food, in-country transportation, attorney fees, and everything else needed to complete this adoption. Thousands of dollars more.

A long, complicated uphill journey still awaited us even after receiving and accepting the referral to finally adopt Juan David. And sadly, I never managed to get through all the red tape to reconnect with him via the telephone. In fact, his own brother couldn't even get permission to contact him. We had no idea what they told him. For all we knew, he probably thought it all fell apart again when I stopped calling.

I prayed for him every day.

The international adoption process is absolutely insane. No family or child should ever go through what we did in order to become a family. Ever.

15

A FINAL BOOST UPWARD

"Consider it pure joy, my brothers, whenever you face trials of many kinds, because you know that the testing of your faith develops perseverance. Perseverance must finish its work so that you may be mature and complete, not lacking anything."

James 1:2–4

From Grief to Joy

I grieved losing you
Almost as if you had died
My heart shattered in pieces
While I did nothing but cry.

He wrapped His arms around me
And walked me to the mirror.

He showed me how with time
His joy replaced my tears.

Those tears led me to seek him
Amidst the trials and the pain.
Countless hours spent with my Lord
Gave me a strength I couldn't feign.

My trials actually helped me
To grow stronger every day.
The joy of seeking Christ
Literally wiped my tears away.

God knew ahead of time what these last few months would do to me. He knew I needed to immerse myself in the Word daily in order to make it through. How fitting to study the book of James[5] in our weekly women's Bible study at the time. I recited the first four verses of the book on a daily basis, adding more verses each day.

"Consider it pure joy . . . because you know that the testing of your faith produces perseverance . . ." I wanted that perseverance to finish its work in me, just like the scripture said.

May brought more waiting as we continued to fight through more tedious parts of the process. Then, to add stress upon stress, our assumed place of lodging fell through. We'd stayed in the same apartment complex for two years and looked forward to feeling at home again, close to many of our good friends. Much to our dismay, though, none of those specific apartments were available for the month of June.

We researched hotels for adoptive families, but the prices were outrageous compared to what we'd planned to pay for an apartment. Plus we felt the apartment would give Juan David a more realistic family experience right away.

Our friend Zayde pointed us to a website for an organization that offers lodging options for only a fraction of the cost of a hotel, personal apartments that people rent out while they travel elsewhere. We found a nice furnished apartment available for a similar rate as the other apartments. But until we got there, I remained leery of the whole concept. Even our attorney seemed nervous. God knew though, and he had us covered.

Timing was everything at this point, and every step from here on out would work like dominoes. Until we had a final date arranged to take custody of Juan David, we couldn't do anything. Once we got it, we needed every last detail covered immediately.

Finally, on Thursday, May 30, our first piece fell into place, causing a domino effect with every other piece. Here is an excerpt from my blog entry that day explaining how precisely each detail connected itself to the previous one.

- Thursday morning—Mike called the agency director, and she told us to go ahead and purchase our tickets so we could start applying for our visas.
- Thursday afternoon—I called our attorney, and he also said to apply for the visas as soon as possible. (We are all in agreement to "assume" our unconfirmed date on the 11th to take custody of Juan David.) We both made arrangements to take the next day off from work to travel to both Austin and Houston before the consulate closed at 2:30 in Houston. I arranged for someone to take David to school in the morning so we could leave at 5 a.m. Then we needed to purchase our tickets because our visa application requires a departure date and length of stay.
- Thursday evening—Mike called the airline to see if they offer discounts for adoptive families. After he spent at

least an hour on the phone and was ready to book the tickets, the guy said, "Oh. You need to book them in person at the airport so you can show legal proof you are adopting." So, Mike received a code to confirm the prices and told the guy we were headed straight to the airport.

◆ Thursday night—We all three jumped in the car and headed to the airport. When we arrived there, we realized we forgot one major detail. We didn't have credit cards, only a debit card with a cap on how much can be debited from our account each day. Our tickets would exceed that. (Insert moment of panic. Remember, we needed our ticket information before leaving at 5 a.m. on Friday, but the bank was already closed, now 8:30 at night.) We called some close friends from church, and they agreed to drive to the airport to meet us with a credit card. Mike went inside, only to find all the ticket counters closed. We couldn't do anything until they opened at 4:00 a.m. the next morning. Mike called the airline back to find out if there was any way to book our tickets over the phone and fax the required documents, but no, you needed to show them in person. We updated our friends (coming with the credit card) on the situation, and they agreed to meet us at the airport the next day at 4 a.m. (Thank God for people who love us and our sons that much.)

◆ Late Thursday night—We headed back home, knowing tomorrow's long day now got even longer. Mike and David headed to bed, while I reviewed the documents again to make sure everything was there and in order. I would hate to make the eight-hour drive from Dallas to Houston and back to find I left something out. I also sent a quick e-mail to our class at church to ask for prayers, and then I finally fell into bed around midnight.

- 2:30 a.m. on Friday—My alarm went off, and we got up quickly to head out by 3:15. David crawled into the truck to keep sleeping.

- 4:00 a.m.—We arrived at the airport, Mike went inside, and our friend soon joined him. They came out again at 5:30 with tickets in hand. Mike raved about the customer service from the lady at the counter. She said hearing our adoption story completely made her day. The adoption discount saved us around $2,000, so having to go in person was worth the inconvenience. Our friend stood with us in the parking lot and prayed for the remainder of our day to go smoothly. David then switched to our friend's vehicle to continue sleeping a bit longer before he fed him and took him to school. We headed straight for Austin.

- 8:30 a.m.—We arrived at the Secretary of State building in Austin with little to no traffic. We quickly filled in the ticket information in the already notarized letter that we needed apostilled at this location. We'd done this before, so we went straight to the office, and they tended to us immediately. Ten minutes later, we began our drive to Houston.

- 11:30 a.m.—We stopped at an office supply store in Houston to make the required copies of our tickets to turn in to the Colombian consulate with our visa applications.

- 12:00 noon—We arrived at the Colombian consulate and took a number. I loved seeing all the pictures on the walls of Colombia, and I embraced the sound of other Colombians speaking. They have a different accent that sounds beautiful to me. We turned in our paperwork but needed to redo our applications because they printed out onto three pages instead of two, and then we waited while the man at the counter reviewed our documents. After about an hour or so, he asked for my contact information and said it would take three days to approve before sending our passports back to us. I reminded him we left on the 8th (eight days away), and he assured us we'd get our passports back before then.

◆ 1:30—We finished! We noticed a business card at the consulate for a Colombian restaurant right outside of Houston, so we headed there for lunch to celebrate.

◆ 2:00—We enjoyed our lunch date together over some delicious Colombian food. We bought David one of his favorite Colombian drinks to take to him, and then we started to head back home.

◆ 3:00—We sent David a text to remind him to ride the bus since he didn't normally ride the bus on Fridays. He went to his friend's house after school and spent a fun evening out with his longtime buddy.

◆ 7:30—We arrived back into town, grabbed a bite for dinner at our favorite local restaurant, and headed home. Exhausted, but totally relieved.

◆ A week from today, we head back to Colombia for the third time. This will be the third year in a row we are leaving for Colombia immediately after school gets out—except this time, we had nothing to do with planning that. I'm sure we'll see more glitches before it's all said and done (remember, we're talking about international adoption). But, we're glad to finally have those tickets in hand.

◆ Tickets in hand. Did I really say that?

Only eight days left until we would board another plane to Colombia, this time to finally take custody of our beloved Juan David. The son we lost and grieved, now soon to be given back.

For good.

During our infamous road trip to Austin and Houston, my phone unexpectedly rang, only hours after purchasing our tickets at the airport.

"Rachelle, I just want you to know that we've decided to award you with a direct grant of $2500 for your adoption expenses. I hear you need the money pretty quickly, so I'm sending the check out in today's mail." The lady's enthusiastic voice made my heart beat even faster. This was the same grant awarded to us (and then lost to us) from our first adoption pursuit. Money we'd raised through the generosity of friends and family four years earlier. I struggled for four years to understand why God burdened our friends' hearts to give only to let us lose every penny of it.

Yet now I saw it. He preserved that specific amount of money to provide for us now.

In addition to the grant, more money appeared in the unlikeliest of places. An unexpected check for $1,000 from a single woman. Another check for $500 from a family who'd already helped us out financially. Even a check for the exact amount we'd just paid to our animal sitter.

Things also worked out well in David's favor now that all the details came together. He didn't miss a single day of school, his fifth-grade graduation, or any of the other fun end-of-school activities. He also achieved his goal of perfect attendance for his entire year of fifth grade, the first year he'd ever done so. His teacher inspired him daily and still stands as one of his greatest role models.

I, too, felt blessed. I didn't need a substitute to cover my class for the last week of school. I brought the year to a close with my students and finished up my year-end duties without having to pass that burden on to a teammate.

Almost there.

At last.

16

A GLIMPSE OF THE MOUNTAIN

"Therefore, since we are surrounded by such a great cloud of witnesses, let us throw off everything that hinders and the sin that so easily entangles, and let us run with perseverance the race marked out for us. Let us fix our eyes on Jesus, the author and perfecter of our faith."

Hebrews 12:1–2a

Forgetting the worries, the fears and the doubts

Answering the moment he calls

Inviting his guidance each step we take

Trusting his plan as better than our own

He is always and completely in control.

Saturday morning. June 8th, 2013. Our flight would take off later that evening. Our third summer trip to Colombia, but this time, I packed for four. Three of us would arrive in Colombia, but four of us would come home.

I never packed for a trip before without knowing when we'd come home. A month might pass. Six weeks. Eight weeks. Our visas, which thankfully arrived in the mail two days before, gave us legal approval to stay for ninety days. I hoped we didn't need to stay for that long, but truthfully, we didn't know. We had to prepare for the possibility.

While our friends drove us to the airport, I got a message online from no one other than Juan David himself. We lost permission to have contact with him in December, but he still managed to connect with me online on a few rare occasions.

He remembered that we visited Colombia in the summers to see his brother, so a few days earlier he sent me a message asking when we were coming and if he could see us. I told him soon and that we'd try. This message was different.

"When exactly are you coming? I need to know exactly when." Hmmm. Did he know yet?

"I told you we will come soon. Why?" I hated playing this game.

"My social worker told me yesterday that I am being adopted on Thursday." Only hours before we boarded our plane, and he finally knew, or so I thought.

"See. I told you we loved you and have always loved you." Oh, to wrap my arms around that boy! I could hardly wait. I didn't realize at that moment he still didn't know who planned to adopt him. He wouldn't know until he finally saw our faces.

We boarded the plane a few hours later for an overnight flight to Colombia, stopping in Atlanta, Georgia, on the way. Thankfully, a friend in Colombia arranged at the last minute for a driver to pick us up at the airport in Bogotá early the next morning, someone trustworthy to take us to our apartment in an unfamiliar part of the city.

The owners of the apartment arranged for an elderly man to meet us with the keys at five in the morning. Everything went smoothly from pick up to the transfer of keys. We found ourselves in a beautiful apartment complex in a safe part of town, and we slept the rest of the morning away before settling in for an indefinite length of stay.

Later that afternoon, we stepped outside to walk around and familiarize ourselves with our surroundings. We also needed to find a place to eat and buy a few groceries. We found a huge mall and grocery store within a ten minute walk down the street, so we headed there.

Before walking into the mall, I caught a quick glimpse of the famous Monserrate tucked into the mountain right in front of us. *The* mountain. The one God used to show me he'd taken us from the mountain, to the valley, and back two years earlier. The one he used to inspire me to write down our journey to Julian in my first book.

Now I could get a glimpse of that very mountain every single day, even from our apartment complex. A daily reminder that God helped us climb back up the mountain . . . again! Oh, how I needed that reminder over the next five and a half weeks.

We hoped for an appointment to reunite with Juan David on Monday, June 10, or Tuesday, June 11. But, shortly after we purchased our tickets and applied for our visas, we received our appointment for Thursday, June 13, at nine in the morning. That meant we had Sunday through Wednesday on our own. It gave us time to get settled, reconnect with old friends, and spend time with Julian. However, Julian and our other friends lived about an hour away from our apartment, so things didn't work out so conveniently.

It did give David time to settle in well before adding Juan David to the mix, so I'm thankful it worked out that way for his sake. Julian came to visit us on Wednesday afternoon after his morning classes and stayed through dinner. I loved catching up with him. Between his school and work schedules, very few opportunities existed for him to even visit with us this year. Quite a difference from the Julian we'd left jobless and almost penniless a year before. The growth I saw in his self-confidence made me so proud of him.

Thursday morning finally arrived, and we patiently waited in a little white room for Juan David and his social worker to walk through the door. When he did arrive, they sent him to another room while his social worker and psychologist transferred important paperwork into our care. School transcripts. Medical and dental reports. Pictures. Memorabilia.

We knew these ladies. We'd met with both of them before. Yet somehow this reunion felt very awkward. We wondered if maybe they found it difficult to say good-bye. After handing me the large envelope and telling us what to expect with Juan David at first, they finally left the room and let him in for that long overdue reunion.

Juan David and I hugged each other for what seemed a very long embrace. A moment forever secured in time. God finally gave him back to me.

He wrapped his arm around David, his new little brother, and we took pictures of our two David's together. He'd grown so much over the last year, so tall and thin now with his hair cut really short. No longer the same little guy with long curls who spent a weekend with us a year ago. All the more reason to thank God for the opportunities we had to see him, know him, and interact with him in those younger years.

Our new son, nearly a young adult now, joined his forever family at the age of fifteen. Thursday, June 13, now occupies the calendar as a reminder of our "Gotcha Day."

Later in the afternoon, I slipped into the bedroom of the apartment to carefully look through the contents of the envelope his social worker gave me. Much to my surprise, I found two little pictures tucked into all of the paperwork. Two colored photographs, the same ones God placed on my computer screen five years earlier, the same pictures I printed and put on our refrigerator to pray for. A little girl and a little boy. She gave me the originals of both of those pictures. Juan David's picture and Viviana's picture, too.

Before the kids leave the orphanage for an adoption, they make a memory book to give to their new parents. Juan David's book contained pictures of a few key events in his life, as well as memories of the orphanage, his schools, and his friends.

I'm sure he treasures all of them, but a certain picture jumped out at me and immediately captured my heart. Three faces joined together in one location. Juan David, Julian, and their beautiful little sister. A picture none of them knew existed.

Juan David will forever be my son, but I consider it a joy and privilege to have also known and loved both of his siblings. The road ahead would be difficult and challenging, but the connections we'd shared to both his brother and sister helped immensely with how quickly we connected as a new family.

The last family he stayed with in Colombia encouraged him to forget his biological siblings, to move on without them. We encouraged him to hold on to them and their memories as tightly as he could. We love them and miss them too.

Besides the connection to Julian and the connection we once had to their sister, God also blessed us with one of the most amazing connections of all. Mercedes. After we visited her the summer before, all of his memories of her role in his life came back to him. He recalls the time he spent in her home as a child, and now he eagerly awaits more opportunities to visit with her whenever we return to Colombia for vacations.

Mercedes invited us to her home again the following Sunday for lunch. Before we ate, God gave me the opportunity to watch my boys play together in the very park where Juan David played as a child and kick the ball around on the same field where he played soccer as a little boy.

She prepared and fed us his favorite foods for lunch, all the while reminiscing about old times with him. He felt right at home. Later he confided in me that she was more of a mom to him than his biological mother ever was. She took care of him, fed him, taught him, and kept him safe.

While the boys played outside again after we ate, Mercedes and I walked to the store where Julian worked to buy some ice cream. On the way, she took me for a walk down memory lane to show me several places where the boys lived as small children, filling in so many missing pieces of information, things I would never find written in any of Juan David's files. Things only she knew about my precious son's childhood.

I am truly blessed to know her. I cherish her friendship, her supportive and loving role in Julian's life, and the spiritual foundation she laid in Juan David's young heart.

17

FINISHING THE CLIMB

"Being confident of this, that he who began a good work in you
will carry it on to completion until the day of Christ Jesus."
Philippians 1:6

Almost There

We're almost finished climbing
Soon we'll make it to the top.
With only a few steps to go
How could we even think to stop?
The road has not been easy.
The climb has not been fun.
But we know you use our journey
To complete what you have begun.

The next few weeks still brought quite a bit of challenge. We'd never spent more than a weekend with Juan David before, so we now needed to adjust to a fourth person (again), a second son, a teenager, and a second language in our family. Not just for a month. For forever.

We filled our first week with fun activities as we began to get to know each other better. We returned to our favorite go-karts and ate at our favorite restaurant. We watched a ton of movies late into the night. For the days we didn't plan activities, we made a schedule to add some structure to the day.

After our first week, we survived our Integration meeting, successfully integrating as a family unit. The adoption was still incomplete, but our custody arrangement was now permanent. In this meeting, another psychologist interviewed Juan David for quite a while, and then she interviewed us. She couldn't get over his level of maturity, despite his circumstances and history. It didn't match other kids his age with a history similar to his.

"He really wants to become a part of your family." She advised us of things we should and shouldn't do because of his unique history, but we all signed to say everything looked good. We had successfully become a family.

In the evening Zayde and her daughter joined us at Monserrate, *back up on the top of the mountain*, to celebrate. We took pictures of the city at night, while it all looked so calm, beautiful, and peaceful. We gave Juan David a small postcard of Dallas at night to welcome him to our family.

Dallas, the city that had called his name for far too long.

Up to this point, all had gone rather well. We loved being in Colombia now with Juan David by our side. We had to type another important document and get it notarized the following morning so Mike could return home on Saturday. We hoped to follow soon, possibly within another two weeks.

Who knew what a mess that one piece of paper could cause, a quick reminder of the differences in our cultures. If we thought paperwork on the U.S. side of the adoption was complicated, we found complication magnified in Colombia. So much for accomplishing more than one task in a day!

We arranged to see Julian once more before he left for work that afternoon, right after getting our paper notarized. It didn't happen. It would have been our only chance to get a family picture with both him and Juan David in it, but we didn't make it in time. Mike's flight left too early the next morning for Julian to join us, so we never took that picture.

I seriously thought we'd manage fine without Mike. We'd miss him, but we had plenty of connections to keep us safe and busy. I spoke the language and he didn't, so I actually even thought it might be easier not having to translate so much of the time.

We gave David the freedom to decide whether to go with Dad or stay with me and Juan David. At first he wanted to go home with Dad, but he liked our apartment so much he decided to stay.

The reality of Mike leaving David with me hit me on the way to the airport. David loves and adores his Daddy. The separation would tear him apart. Sure enough, the tears came as soon as Mike checked in. We calmed him down with his favorite breakfast, just long enough for Mike to slip away.

The boys and I raced home to our apartment balcony to watch Mike's plane take off, thus beginning the most challenging three and a half weeks with a miserable little boy who desperately missed his Daddy.

I, too, found myself incredibly homesick just a week later. I missed Mike terribly. I also missed my car, so tired of riding in overpriced taxis and overcrowded buses.

All of our friends, including Julian and Mercedes, lived too far away to make visiting convenient for anyone. The travel to and from their homes exhausted me, both physically and financially, plus David's little body couldn't handle all the change.

He suffered with horrible tummy aches at random times in the day, putting him in tears, along with extreme headaches from the altitude. He carried his water bottle (with purified water) everywhere he went, but he still found himself dehydrated way too much. As much as we wanted to see our friends, the physical toll on David's little body wasn't worth it.

By the end of June, our lawyer said everything had been approved; now we waited on "*sentencia*," the day we could officially sign the adoption decree.

Rather than wait by the phone each day, we accepted an invitation to join Zayde and her family on a vacation to a famous little town called Villa de Leyva in a beautiful part of the country called Boyacá. We heard wonderful things about it, so we welcomed the opportunity to get out of the city.

Julian obtained permission from work to spend the entire week with us. Due to his complicated work and school schedule, we'd only seen him three times by this point in our trip, so I looked forward to spending some quality time with him. I also wanted to give him this gift of time with his brother, knowing the heartache that awaited him once Juan David left Colombia without him. Our attorney liked the idea of us experiencing more of the rich beauty Colombia has to offer outside of the city.

Five or six days with some friends in a more peaceful environment would do all of us some good. I hated being a single parent for the last eight days, so I couldn't wait to have Julian around and to be in the company of other adults. Julian could spend quality time with Juan David, giving me some quality time with David. Every day without his Daddy got harder and harder.

On the way to Villa de Leyva, we stopped at a historical landmark to take pictures and at a well-known *arepa* factory (a traditional pancake-like food specifically from that part of the country). Our trip started off great until that nasty tummy ache threatened to spin David out of control. He either cried or lashed out at me violently in reaction to the extreme pain.

That was only the start. I should have known something was terribly wrong.

Once we made it to our destination and settled in to a beautiful "hotel" used only for Christian gatherings, David seemed to feel better after he rested in bed. Lots of fun shopping trips and tourist activities awaited us, including an unforgettable ride on horseback to fully experience the rich beauty of this town. We also took the kids swimming in a place called Pozos Azules, man-made ponds of clear, blue water.

Mike called us every night, hating the fact that he couldn't share this experience in Colombia with us.

Friday, our last day there, held a full day of plans. Zayde arranged for us to rent a large van and driver for the day so all nine of us could travel together, and she coordinated an all-day trip to visit several other well-known places within Boyacá. We split the cost to rent the van, and we all went to bed early in order to eat breakfast and leave by 5:30 in the morning.

The next day, David woke up as chipper as could be, ready for a fun day. He went to wake up Juan David and Julian, but the color soon left his cheeks.

"I don't feel so good, Mommy." He complained that his stomach hurt and he felt like throwing up.

Zayde said she woke up feeling the same stomach symptoms, but she already started to feel better. We figured David had the same temporary problem, so we continued to get ready. He refused to eat breakfast, though, and when I went to check on him, I found him crying on the floor of the bathroom, saying he felt like throwing up.

"I don't want to go anywhere today." He just laid there on the bathroom floor, his face wet with tears. I helped him back into bed to see if he might fall asleep.

Still assuming he had the same minor tummy issues as Zayde, we bundled him up with a blanket and pillow and encouraged him to try to sleep in the van. Within the first thirty minutes of travel, the pain grew worse. He cried into his pillow for the next hour.

Eventually he threw up all over the floor of the van and onto a new hat he'd just bought as a souvenir. We stopped to clean up and then found a little restaurant to get him some broth to help settle his tummy. He refused to eat, though, and when I reached out to hug him, he just cried.

"I miss Daddy." He buried his head into me while my clothing soaked up his tears.

I started to fall apart. Zayde kept telling me I needed to stay strong for David, but I knew something had to be terribly wrong. He suffered from tummy aches all month that kept getting worse. I felt like a horrible mother for not taking them more seriously.

Zayde asked David if he could make it a little bit farther so we could enjoy the day together at a place with hot springs to swim in, or if he wanted to find an emergency clinic close by. She warned him the clinic would take several hours, but he still opted for the clinic.

My poor baby! What had I done?

Because of the legal situation with Juan David, I couldn't let him continue to travel with our friends without me. He stayed with us at the clinic, so Julian chose to stay with us too. The rest of the crew continued on to the hot springs, assuring us they'd come back later in the day to pick us up. We were about three hours from Villa de Leyva in a little town Juan David shared a last name with, a last name he could only claim for another week or so until he officially took our last name.

As soon as a staff member checked David into a little room at the clinic and we discussed his symptoms, the doctor thought he probably had a gastrointestinal infection. They drew blood and took a urine sample just to be sure.

The blood results came back showing severe dehydration. They hooked my little boy up to an IV to pump him with electrolytes and give him something for the pain.

"I don't want to die!" David's fear of the IV tore my heart in pieces. His fear only compounded my own.

The pain didn't seem to go away, even an hour or two later. The doctor ordered to keep him under observation for several more hours because of concerns of possible appendicitis. We'd need to wait six hours from the time of the first blood test to take another one.

Six solid hours watching my little boy suffer, hoping and praying we didn't need to transfer him to a hospital for surgery in the middle of nowhere that evening.

Julian and Juan David stayed in the little waiting room for the entire day with nothing to eat and nothing to do besides watch whatever played on the TV. Both of them tried several times to come back and see us, but the guard kept kicking them out. Apparently, they allowed only one person to stay in the room with the patient: me.

My cell phone battery had very little life left. I didn't have any way to contact Mike. I couldn't reach my friends. The place was incredibly unsanitary, and I had already used all of the sanitizer I carried in my purse.

I left all of my important custody paperwork back in the room at Villa de Leyva because I didn't want anything to happen to it. I had no way to prove my parental relationship to Juan David if I needed to.

Since we had nothing to eat, I sent the boys to find a store nearby to pick up some food and to an internet cafe to contact Mike via the internet so he could call us. I've never felt so terrified and desperately alone.

After Julian got in touch with him, Mike called every hour to check on us. We couldn't talk long in order to preserve my cell phone battery for as long as possible. He called on all of our prayer warriors to start praying for David. I prayed all day long, but I also dealt with anger toward God for letting my little boy continue to suffer.

David drifted in and out of sleep all day. One of the times he woke up, he saw me crying.

"Mommy, God has a plan. There's a reason this is happening. Something good is going to come out of this." Wow. God used my young son's faith, in the midst of his own pain, to strengthen me.

Zayde and her husband, Alvaro, stayed in contact with Julian throughout the day. In fact, they already made several contacts in an attempt to find the best way to transport David back to Bogotá in the case of a necessary surgery.

I can't even describe the utter elation David and I both felt, though, when the nurse came back with the results of his second blood test.

"He does not have appendicitis. The electrolytes have helped all of his levels improve greatly, so it must be a bacterial infection in his intestines." She, too, had relief written all over her face.

The doctor put him on a very strict diet and prescribed an electrolyte solution for him to take every day. He also wrote a prescription for an antibiotic and pain medication. Zayde and Alvaro returned right as they released David, so we quickly began the drive back to our vacationing rooms in Villa de Leyva.

The next morning, I woke up early and walked down to the courtyard to spend some quiet time with God. I pray a prayer for my boys every day out of Stormie Omartian's, *A Book of Prayer*.[6] I turned back to the prayer I prayed for them the day before.

"I pray that he will have faith strong enough to lift him above his circumstances and limitations and instill in him the confidence of knowing that everything will work together for good."

I thought back to the way David comforted me in that little room at the clinic. God answered my prayer. I was the one falling apart, and David's faith stood the test, exactly as I prayed for him. Sometimes God answers so clearly it gives me goose bumps.

We took a bus to return to Bogotá that evening, hoping to hear good news about our adoption so we could go home soon. After the emotional stress of David's illness, I wanted to go home more than anything. David still needed several days of rest and recovery, though, and we were about to enter into a new whirlwind of events and activity in order to finally take Juan David home with us.

Our case sat approved and ready, but we still waited for the judge to put his final seal on it so we could sign it. Our attorney hoped for Wednesday, so he gave me the address of where to meet him when the time came.

"Be ready to go at a moment's notice."

My nerves got the better of me, as well as a touch of what David had suffered the previous week. Every day I felt more desperate to head home.

I found myself quite discouraged by late morning on Thursday, still waiting on that phone call from my attorney. I lay down to take a nap for the remainder of the morning. David woke me up at 12:30, and the lawyer called fifteen minutes later.

"Come now!" He made sure I had the correct address and then hung up.

"Boys! Get your shoes on. We have to leave right away!" I brushed my hair, and we all three scrambled out of the apartment as quickly as possible.

That afternoon, July 11, 2013, I signed the adoption decree, officially making Juan David our son. We celebrated in the afternoon at our favorite restaurant, and then I stayed in bed the rest of the evening, barely able to keep anything I ate in me.

We still had so much left to do before we could even think of going home. I hoped my stomach issues would clear up soon.

We met our attorney incredibly early the next day to get Juan David's new birth certificate made, wait for the information to appear in the system, get a new ID card, and then apply for his new passport with his new name.

The attorney left his assistant to wait several hours with us for the new ID card, while he went to the Adoptions Office to retrieve Juan David's old passport from his first trip to the States in 2008. He went through every single passport, one by one, two times. He found every other child's passport from that year, except Juan David's. Somehow, someone did not follow procedure to put it where it belonged, and now we were in trouble.

How in the world could they issue Juan David a new passport without turning in the old one? I read worry all over our attorney's face when he returned to tell me about our unique predicament.

He asked to talk to the main person in charge at the Passport Office, but she was not available. They offered for him to talk with several other people, but he insisted he needed to speak with her. She finally came out to let him explain what happened, and relief quickly replaced the worry on his face when she agreed to issue the new passport anyway.

"Only God." He pulled me aside to tell me what he really thought. I loved that we shared the same faith and could talk about it openly.

By that night, my nerves had calmed quite a bit, and the boys, especially David, took good care of me. I finally started feeling better and found myself able to eat again.

Colombia still held us for a few more days, but we'd only rented our apartment until Monday, July 15, and someone already rented it for the following two weeks. We cleaned and packed all day Saturday. Zayde and Alvaro opened up their own small apartment to let us stay with them until we could finally return home. We turned in the keys to the apartment and moved in with them on Sunday evening. May God richly bless them for their hospitality.

Monday morning, we met our attorney again at the Adoptions Office to sign another paper. I just needed to proofread it and sign it so we could head out to take care of other last-minute details. I found an incorrect date on the paper, and of course, nobody could find the original document with the correct date.

After I made a few frantic phone calls, the director of our international adoption agency found a copy of the document we needed and scanned it to me several hours later. I marched it right back into the Adoptions Office, and they corrected the error. I signed it, and we left. So much for saving our last bit of money after all of those taxi rides!

That same day, we went back to the Passport Office to pick up Juan David's new passport, returned to the Embassy doctor to pick up the results from his medical exam, delivered our *sentencia* to our translator, and our attorney requested our appointment with the US Embassy so we could get Juan David's visa to go home. We all assumed we'd get an appointment on Tuesday, so Mike booked us on the midnight flight for Tuesday night.

So close, yet I still felt so far away.

Julian came to say good-bye Tuesday morning. Leaving him behind broke my heart. I knew it broke his, too. We'd spent so little time with him this year, but we loved seeing how he'd grown and matured over the year. God had his hand on Julian, continuing to take care of him and provide him with opportunities to study and work.

Much to our dismay, though, the US Embassy scheduled our appointment for 2:00 in the afternoon on Wednesday, instead of Tuesday. No midnight flight home after all. My heart sank. We went to the Embassy, anyway, without an appointment, but they refused to let us in.

Mike canceled our flights that night and booked us for the midnight flight on Wednesday instead.

Our bags sat packed and ready to go at Zayde and Alvaro's apartment while we headed to the U.S. Embassy Wednesday. First the man behind the counter at the Embassy fingerprinted Juan David. He then looked at me to explain what to expect after that. "It might take a little while for his prints to go through the system, maybe thirty minutes to an hour at the most."

Over two hours later, he called us back to the window to present Juan David with his immigrant visa.

This time all three of us jumped for joy!

"We're coming home!" David screamed into the phone when Mike called shortly after we walked out of the Embassy.

Three hours later, after a rather rushed good-bye to Zayde and Alvaro, we left for the airport. Fortunately, we didn't face a single issue with our paperwork there.

Juan David didn't sleep the entire first flight. He watched movies and listened to music the whole way to Atlanta. As soon as he stepped off the plane in Atlanta on Thursday morning, July 18, 2013, he automatically became a citizen of the United States.

Juan David Alspaugh. Now a Colombian American. Forever our son.

A few hours later, we landed in Dallas, the city that had called his name for years. Mike welcomed all three of us with wide, open arms.

We finally made it home. Two days shy of Colombia's Independence Day, five solid years since the day we first met Juan David back in 2008.

The next day, David left for church camp, embracing the chance to chill out with one of his best friends for the next five days while Juan David settled into his new home.

A new room. Bathroom. House. Pets. Climate. A whole new life. I even took him shopping for a new wardrobe.

Amidst all the unfamiliar surroundings, he found pictures of himself and his biological siblings all over the walls in his new home. Something familiar and comforting, even if the rest of his world had changed.

Always a part of him. Always a part of us.

18

EMPTY NO MORE

"Woman, you have great faith! Your request is granted."
Matthew 15:28

The Empty Room

Four simple walls and a floor
Yet what a story they've contained.
Many dreams have come and gone,
Yet your empty room remained.

First envisioned as a nursery
Yet the baby never came.
Later it became an area
For a puzzle or a game.

A guest room, a library,
An office with space to organize.
A place to store our junk
And miscellaneous supplies.

Then we saw her precious face
And "knew" the room belonged to her.
Soon it filled with dolls and toys
And awaited both her and a brother.

Yet time went by, she didn't come
The room sat empty once again.
A room that held such hope and promise
Now only held tears and pain.

A place to cry, a room to grieve
A space to sit alone with God and pray.
We emptied all the contents,
Gave almost all her stuff away.

"Move on. Let go."
Though we listened, and we tried.
God kept your story moving forward.
His guidance couldn't be denied.

As each year passed before us,
We found more reason to hold on.
Letting go was not an option.
Your presence wasn't gone.

Though your room stayed empty,
It held a continuing story within.
Your pictures soon reoccupied the walls,
Promise resided there once again.

Your sister's vibrant personality lived there,
Then your brother's tender heart moved in.
They both prepared the room to welcome you
To a place you all three had been.

When I walk into that room
And see you asleep on your bed,
Emotions overwhelm me.
Have you risen from the dead?

To see you in your sister's room
With your brother's artwork on the wall.
Your story sitting on the shelf
Doesn't even begin to tell it all.

Only God knows how many tears fell
In a space that once held such gloom
While he tenderly prepared your future
In that simple, empty room.

Empty No More

Life sure did get busy
Once you finally arrived.
You took so well to everything,
You've blossomed, and you've thrived.

It feels as if we're running
Keeping up with both you boys.
You fit right in so naturally
And added your own noise.

It's as if you've always been here,
Or at least were always meant to be.

Yet sometimes I still look your way
And can't believe it's you I see.

I still remember grieving
As if I'd experienced your death.
Now that you're actually here,
It's like you've risen from the dead.

Into your room I walk each morning
To wake you from your sleep.
While I recall so many mornings there
When I could only cry to God and weep.

Your room first awaited a baby,
Who now awaits us all in heaven.
Then we prepared it for your sister
Back when she was only seven.

It later became my meeting room
Where God drew me close each day.
Your carpet still holds my tears,
Your walls guard all the words I prayed.

With time your brother's heart moved in.
His artwork soon occupied the room.
Your newest pictures found a frame.
New hopes emerged from my heart's tomb.

All three of you resided there,
Though empty the room remained.
Until much to everyone's surprise,
Your homecoming would be regained.

Another year of questions,
Yet another chance to try.

A chance to finally see
God answer my first why.

Now I can't help but glance at you
And feel my heart nearly erupt.
God finally filled your room,
And overflowed my cup.

Psalm 23:5—"My cup overflows."

His own room.

A room filled with his brother's artwork on the walls. His sister's favorite color painted on the light switch. A poster-size photo of Bogotá, taken from the top of the mountain. A book on the shelf telling the first part of his journey to our family.

His own bed.

He absolutely loved his new bed. Set up high with several pillows and a big, fluffy comforter. At first he struggled to fall asleep, too full of energy. Now with a little music, he falls asleep easily and sleeps all night, late into the morning if I let him.

Emotions still overwhelm me when I walk into his room. The empty room. The extra room. His sister's room. My exercise room. My prayer room. The room that held my tears. The walls that heard my cries.

I prayed my way through grief while meeting with God every day in that empty room. I begged God to use my broken heart for his glory, somehow.

My daily prayer cards held verses and written prayers such as these two that I used from Beth Moore's book, *Praying God's Word.*[7]

Matthew 15:28—"Lord, I want to be like the one to whom you have said, 'Woman, you have great faith! Your request is granted.' Flourish this kind of faith in me, God!" (p. 45, *Praying God's Word*).

Philippians 1:12–14—"Lord, after this suffering, let it be said that what has happened to me has really served to advance the gospel. As a result, make my Savior clear to all those around me. Because of my suffering and willing perseverance, cause others to be encouraged to speak the Word of God more courageously and fearlessly" (p.211, *Praying God's Word*).

We didn't meet those kids by chance. God orchestrated our first meeting. It all happened for a purpose. We miss Julian, but he remains a solid part of all of our lives. Other doors opened for him to pursue higher education and to travel. God allowed him to be a hero for his brother.

When I walk into Juan David's room now, I can't help but see all five years of the journey to him written all over the walls. Yet I see Juan David in that bed each morning, and I am reminded of the precious gift God gave back to me.

The process to bring him home was harder than I ever imagined. The rest of our journey will last a lifetime, never ceasing to challenge us.

Cultures clash, and languages compete. Adolescence rebels, while independence fights. Voices raise, and tempers erupt. Secrets hide, and trust crumbles. Age lies, while a child remains buried inside at times.

Siblings disagree, and personalities rub. Arrogance denies reality and pushes away affection. Choices overwhelm. Attachment meets resistance.

You never know what event might trigger a memory, for any of us. Nurturing a teenager who already thought he had life figured out is anything but easy.

But love conquers so many negatives, and in most cases, it eventually wins.

I used to sit in church singing choruses with a deep longing in my heart for God to reveal His purpose for our pain. Now I sit in the same church, singing the same choruses, but I hear my son's voice sing them with me.

A reminder that God did indeed reveal his plan and bring it to completion. He took the broken pieces of all of our lives and did more than I could ever dream.

"Now to him who is able to do immeasurably more than all we ask or imagine, according to his power that is at work within us" (Eph. 3:20).

For us.

For Juan David. For Julian. For Viviana.

And for the millions of other orphan voices I hope you heard throughout our story. No one should ever have to face life without a family, no matter how old they are.

An Orphan No more

Everything changed for all of us
I still can hardly believe it's true.
For the first time in years,
I didn't spend Christmas missing you.

We sat side by side in church,
Sang carols by candlelight.
So grateful I was to watch you
Open our gifts to you that night.

I find myself always watching now,
Like I'm on the outside looking in.
Observing every little thing you do,
Studying your every reaction.

What has meant the most to you
Your very first Christmas here?

What goes through your mind
When you no longer see an orphan in the mirror?

How did it feel to see your name
Written on those gifts beneath the tree,
Knowing you're no longer one of the many,
Now you're just part of our family?

How did it feel to give gifts
To a brother, mom, and dad?
How did it feel to make choices
With the spending money you had?

I wonder how it felt for you
To be home for Christmas this year.
I know for me it felt priceless
To finally have you so near.

Epilogue

Shortly after coming home, I taught a women's Bible study for the fall semester at church called *Missing Pieces*,[8] by Jennifer Rothschild, while at the same time I read my friend, Mary DeMuth's, new book, *The Wall Around Your Heart*.[9] Though both were written from very different perspectives and in very different formats, I learned the same main point.

People hurt us. People let us down. Even God seems to let us down. Each hurt, insult, disappointment, or loss leaves us with a hole, a missing piece. We don't understand. We can't make sense of it. We can reach for the bricks to start building up a wall of security around our hearts, protecting ourselves from being hurt like that again. Or we can bend our knees with hands held high in surrender, knowing God, in his sovereignty, allows us to suffer through the emptiness of each piece in order to beckon us to himself. He wants to fill each empty space with another part of himself and his character.

Jennifer Rothschild used a cut-up blanket as an illustration of our faith, showing all the ugly holes left in our blanket that only God can fill. In the study with the women at my church, I, too, cut up a blanket to show specific holes that appeared in my faith over the years, and I shared personally how God filled them in different ways each time. Sometimes he showed me he had something different in mind to fit the hole better than I thought. Other times he showed me that what I saw as several individual holes, he saw as one big hole needing to grow more until it was big enough to hold what he had to give me in its place.

As I shared in my first book, *Unexpected Tears*, despite all the ways God already filled so many missing pieces in my faith, our failed adoption attempt left my faith with a huge, gaping hole—so big I could do nothing but cling to God in desperation to help me understand. In so doing, I found him in many more ways than I ever knew I needed him.

Years later, Juan David finally came home. It all made sense. He was the missing piece, right? Surely he fit all the right dimensions and held just the right shape to fit the hole that formed when he didn't come home the first time. It made complete sense until I reread what I'd written in my first book in the fall of 2011, retelling my thoughts as I stood at the top of the mountain, overlooking the city of Bogotá, Colombia with Julian at my side.

"I could finally see now how intricately God worked together every tiny detail. The pieces of our puzzle all fit together without a single piece missing" (*Unexpected Tears*, p. 177).

God had already filled that gaping hole in my blanket of faith. So where did Juan David fit? He fit right in that added measure of faith God had already tagged onto my blanket. My faith grew and stretched beyond what I ever expected, creating a spot for the extra pieces, not the missing ones.

And so our journey of faith continues, adding one extra piece at a time.

Appendix
A LIFE WITH PURPOSE

As you read about my family's journey through a painful adoption experience, I hope you gleaned an even deeper message written between the lines of our story. *Nothing matters more than a personal relationship with Jesus Christ.*

Living through a "failed" adoption happened to be the circumstance God used in our lives to show us that he never leaves us, whether we find ourselves on the mountaintop or in the valley. He fills our lives with meaning and purpose. He satisfies our hearts when we stop looking everywhere else for fulfillment.

If you read through my story and felt drawn to begin your own relationship with Christ, please know you can do so at this very moment. *Call out to him. Admit your need for him. Surrender your life to him.* We all fall short of his glory, but Jesus Christ (God's son) already paid the price for the sins that separated us from him. His salvation is a gift, one we can never earn, no matter how hard we try. We can't fix ourselves on our own, but if we give our life to him, he does the fixing, drawing us closer and closer to himself to make us more like him.

By confessing our sin, admitting we need a Savior, and giving our life to Jesus, we can enter into a relationship with the God who created us. We can find assurance that he will prepare a place for us in Heaven for eternity, but we can also find an abundant and meaningful life here and now. A life with purpose.

Imagine a life with such an awesome relationship. I can't even begin to imagine a life without it. Without him.

How can I begin a relationship with God?
Believe the following:

◆ Christ makes us a new creation. "Therefore, if anyone is in Christ, he is a new creation. The old has passed away; behold, the new has come" (2 Cor. 5:17, ESV). Tell God you want him to change you into a new creation to bring honor to him.

◆ God forgives our sins and allows us a new start. "Blessed are those whose lawless deeds are forgiven, and whose sins are covered" (Rom. 4:7, ESV). Let God know you know you are a sinner and want his forgiveness.

◆ He grants us eternal life. "For God so loved the world, that he gave his only Son, that whoever believes in him should not perish but have eternal life" (John 3:16, ESV). Ask God to give you eternal life by allowing you into his family.

◆ God gives us indescribable joy. "Though you have not seen him, you love him. Though you do not now see him, you believe in him and rejoice with joy that is inexpressible and filled with glory, obtaining the outcome of your faith, the salvation of your souls" (1 Pet. 1:8–9). This doesn't promise happiness, but joy in knowing Christ as your personal savior, and hope that he manages the details of our lives for his glory.

◆ We can begin talking to God about all aspects of our life. We can ask him to show us which paths to take or what decisions to make, and start communicating even the tiny details of our lives with him. But let's not forget to listen. God wants to speak back.

◆   God talks to us through the Bible, so start reading his
     message to you. Websites such as BibleGateway.com
     or YouVersion.com offer a variety of translations free of
     charge. I recommend beginning with the Gospel of John
     or one of the other Gospels to learn what Jesus taught
     during his time on earth.

◆   Authenticity Book House would love to hear about your
     decision to follow Christ. E-mail us at info@abhbooks.
     com. We would love to pray for you and celebrate with
     you the new life you have in Christ.

Endnotes

1 *Experiencing God—Knowing and Doing the Will of God*, Henry and Richard Blackaby and Claude King, 2007, Life Way Press.

2 *Interrupción Divina: Como transitar lo inesperado*, Priscilla Shirer, 2011, B&H Español (*Divine Interruption: Navigating the Unexpected*).

3 *Children of the Day* Member Workbook, Beth Moore, 2014, LifeWay Press.

4 *Esther—It's Tough Being a Woman*, Beth Moore, 2008, Life Way Press.

5 *James: Mercy Triumphs*, Beth Moore, 2008, Life Way Press.

6 *A Book of Prayer*, Stormie Omartian, 2006, The Power of a Praying Parent series, Harvest House Publishers.

7 *Praying God's Word*, Beth Moore, 2000, Broadman and Holman Publishers.

8 *Missing Pieces—Real Hope Shen Life Doesn't Make Sense*, Jennifer Rothschild, 2012, Life Way Press.

9 *The Wall Around Your Heart—Mary DeMuth*, 2013, Thomas Nelson.

About the Author

Rachelle D. Alspaugh seldom finds herself at a loss for words when she writes. She tells stories about faith, and her poetry often springs from real events in her life.

Rachelle yearns to help orphans. She enjoys traveling, especially when her travels intersect with her passion for missions. In college, she went to Buenos Aires for a semester as an exchange student. She also spent two months in Mexico as a summer missionary and has taken several mission trips to Mexico since.

Rachelle teaches Bilingual Education in a public school system just outside of Dallas, Texas, where she lives with her husband and two sons, along with their two dogs and two cats. She also enjoys teaching women's Bible studies at her church.

"Trust in the Lord with all your heart and lean not on your own understanding; in all your ways, acknowledge him and he will make your paths straight."
Proverbs 3:5 – 6

THE MINISTRY OF ABH

Authenticity Book House is a nonprofit publishing ministry that:

- Serves gifted Christian authors by removing publishing barriers.
- Equips non-English speaking pastors and teachers with biblical literature in their heart languages.
- Employs skilled believers in developing nations.

Serving Aspiring Authors

- Authors own all copyrights.
- ABH absorbs all costs for cover design, editing, formatting, proofreading, translating, and marketing of the author's first three books.
- ABH does not take any royalties on sales of the author's first three books.

Equipping Pastors Worldwide

- 20 percent of net royalties on all ABH books goes to support international pastors.
- ABH targets strategic language groups that lack biblical resources.

Empowering Believers

- ABH selects authors with confirmed Christlike character and ministry effectiveness.
- ABH employs translators and editors around the globe.

Please help us glorify Christ in editorial excellence. If you find a mistake in this book, please e-mail the error and the page number to quality@abhbooks.com.

www.ingramcontent.com/pod-product-compliance
Lightning Source LLC
LaVergne TN
LVHW051056080426
835508LV00019B/1905